POSTCARDS
from
SANTA CLAUS

Robert C. Hoffman

SEP   2003

SQUAREONE
PUBLISHERS

MUNDY BRANCH LIBRARY - O.C.P.L.
1204 S. GEDDES ST.
SYRACUSE, NEW YORK 13204

Cover Design: Phaedra Mastrocola
In-House Editing: Marie Caratozzolo
Consultant: George J. Lankevich
Interior Design: Phaedra Mastrocola
Typesetting: Gary A. Rosenberg

Square One Publishers | Garden City Park, NY 11040 | **516-535-2010** | www.squareonepublishers.com

Library of Congress Cataloging-in-Publication Data

Hoffman, Robert C., 1946—
    Postcards from Santa Claus : sights & sentiments from the last
century / Robert C. Hoffman.
        p. cm.
Includes index.
    ISBN 0-7570-0105-X (quality phk.)
    1, Santa Claus—History. 2. Santa Claus—History—Pictorial.
works. I. Title.
    GT4992 .H64 2002
    394.2663—dc21

                                                    2001005184.

Copyright © 2002 by Robert C. Hoffman

All rights reserved. No part of this publication may be reproduced, stored in a retrieval system, or transmitted, in any form or by any
means, electronic, mechanical, photocopying, recording, or otherwise, without the prior written permission of the copyright owner.

Printed in the United States of America

10 9 8 7 6 5 4 3 2 1

Contents

Dedicated with delight
to
Hannah Shultz and Gavin Davis

Acknowledgments

For their contributions to this project, I offer my sincere appreciation to Rudy Shur, Marie Caratozzolo, Lane Davis, William Nolan, John Ignizio, George Lankevich, and Joanne Abrams. I would also like to thank my father, "Santa Del," and friend Hans Tanner for their continuing support and encouragement. A special thank-you, as always, goes to my wife, Joan, whose love, friendship, and compassion mean everything to me, and to my daughters, Amy and Julie, for always believing in Santa Claus.

$\mathbb{I}$ntroduction

$\mathbb{L}$ ike most people, I can vividly remember my childhood and the excitement I always felt during the Christmas season—the most wonderful time of the year. The air seemed charged as the holiday neared, and everyone fussed for days to help usher in the celebration. There was nothing like it, especially for my younger brother and me.

Our home was transformed into a warm and cozy wonderland. A freshly cut Douglas fir stood poised in the living room, trimmed with colored lights and precious generations-old ornaments; garlands outlined mantles and window ledges; mistletoe hung over doorways; and fiery logs popped and crackled in the fireplace. The tantalizing smell of my mother's freshly baked cookies and holiday breads filled the air. It was a time of visits from friends, long-distance phone calls, and happy family gatherings (even Grumpy Uncle Henry seemed delightful). I loved it all . . . the sights and smells, the family and friends. But, nothing was more exciting than the anticipation of Santa Claus' magical visit.

Santa Claus—that mystical gift-giving fellow whose very name evokes the spirit of the season—is one of the holiday's most beloved icons. He toils all year in his North Pole workshop, creating toys and gifts for good little girls and boys the world over. It's not known how he does it, but each year, children awaken wide-eyed on Christmas morning to discover the special gifts he has left for them under the tree. He travels the world round in a sleigh led by eight magical reindeer, yet has never actually been seen.

Postcards from Santa Claus offers a unique and fascinating look at this beloved legendary figure. Through beautiful postcard images and personal messages that span over a century, this book chronicles the history of Santa—from his earliest appearance in the 1800s to the present day. You'll meet Saint Nicholas, the generous fourth-century Catholic bishop who served as the inspiration for Santa Claus, as well as other gift-giving figures in countries throughout the world. You will also see how Santa has evolved over time, influenced by war, politics, and Madison Avenue. Fat, thin, serious, happy, colorful, drab, and, of course, mysterious, Santa has changed, perhaps even as we have changed, depending on the world's mood and social condition.

Precursors to Christmas cards, beautifully produced holiday postcards had their origins in Germany and Austria-Hungary in the late 1800s.

NATIONAL SANTA CLAUS SERIES

1998

COPYRIGHT 1907 ULLMAN MFG. CO. N. Y.

UNITED STATES

By 1905, postcards of all types were being sold in America by the millions. Holiday cards were commonly used to send greetings of the season to friends and family both nearby and in countries back home. And, as you will see, Santa's image is one that has been a popular choice for gracing the fronts of these cards, no matter where they were produced. A universally loved figure, Santa belongs to everyone—to people of all countries.

The collection of postcards presented in this book will take you on a historic journey of this "jolly old elf," mapping out images of Santa as they have been reflected in six major time periods. The book opens with the Victorian "Turn-of-the-Century Santa," covering the years of the late 1800s, and then moves on to the glory days of the postcard from 1900 to 1919, when "Santa Comes of Age." During the period from 1920 to 1940, postcards chronicle "Santa Between the Wars," and in "Santa Goes to War," they show the important role he played from 1941 to 1945. During the postwar years, when the country's buying power was unleashed, "Santa Met the Baby Boomers," and stepped squarely into the world of commercialism. The book concludes with "Modern-Day Santa," spanning the period from 1965 to the millennium. In each chapter, the cards—both foreign and domestic—and their messages reveal Santa's changing image over the past century.

In addition to the parade of postcards, fascinating insets throughout the book highlight Santa trivia and interesting holiday features. You'll discover the origin of the Santa legend, as well as popular traditions of the season; the creators of the Santa we know today; how Christmas is celebrated throughout Europe; Santa's popular role in film and music, and so much more.

I have written *Postcards from Santa Claus* for anyone who loves Santa and the spirit of Christmas as much as I do. My hope is that you will derive many hours of pleasure paging through it, as it is sure to evoke wonderful holiday memories all year long.

Postcards from Santa Claus

CHAPTER ONE

Turn-of-the-Century Santa 1880–1899

Santa Claus—primarily a creation of nineteenth-century America—has roots that can be traced back as far as the fourth century to Saint Nicholas, a Catholic bishop who was noted for his generous nature and legendary good deeds. But, as discussed in "Images of Santa Claus," beginning on page 95, during the time of the Protestant Reformation, this popular Christmas figure was viewed as being too closely associated with the Catholic Church. Thus, many countries throughout the world began creating more secular figures as their season's traditional gift givers.

In America, Clement Clarke Moore's 1823 poem, "A Visit From St. Nicholas" (page 17), described a Saint Nick with a new look. Gone was any semblance of the tall, thin saint of yore with his long brown robe and pointed hat. In his place, Moore presented a miniaturized Saint Nick who was plump and jolly and flew over rooftops in a tiny reindeer-driven sleigh. It was an image that was later picked up and further developed by German-born political cartoonist Thomas Nast. Between 1862 and 1886, Nast created annual drawings of Santa Claus for *Harper's Weekly*. Gone were any religious characteristics of Saint Nicholas, and, inspired by Moore's poem, Nast drew a never-before-seen figure called Santa Claus—a warm and endearing grandfatherly gent, who smoked a pipe and carried a pack full of toys. It was the first drawing of this joyful little man, and it didn't take long for him to become our friend.

The Victorian period also marked the beginning of Santa's image on postcards, trade cards, magazines, calendars, children's books, and newspaper advertisements. His pleasing appearance was both refreshing and new, and he was a perfect match for the cherubic children, gentle animals, and beautiful angels with whom he appeared. Postcards bearing pictures of Santa were used for business correspondence and product promotion, as well as holiday greetings. It was the first time, other than in newspapers or on company display ads, that Santa was used to endorse products. And he proved to be a natural salesman.

Santa was also a familiar sight on trade cards. Similar in size and shape to postcards, trade cards served as another early form of advertising. A printing process called *chromolithography* gave them, as well as European-produced postcards, outstanding color, and many bore the illustrations of well-known artists of the day, such as Kate Greenaway and Maude Humphrey. When compared to postcards, the trade cards' main drawback was that they came in a variety of sizes and had to be placed in envelopes before they were mailed.

The final decades of nineteenth-century America were characterized by a tremendous flood of immigrants. As millions of people entered the country, they were eager to send word of their safe arrival to loved ones back home. Inexpensive or even free, postcards were available to fill this immediate need. And during the Christmas season, holiday postcards were mailed back and forth across the sea in enormous numbers. Different representations of Santa from countries all over the world were eagerly sent and joyfully received.

Fueled by the power of a growing immigrant labor force, as well as the influence of the Industrial Revolution, new businesses began to emerge along with the promise of improved wages and the prospect of disposable income. Increasing numbers of factory-made products were designed to help make life easier during the late 1800s. Items such as sewing machines, typewriters, and lawnmowers began flooding the marketplace, and people were interested in buying them. Postcards with Santa soliciting these and other "must-have" products became commonplace. After all, Santa was everyone's trusted friend, so if he appeared with a product, it had to be good. Storeowners loved Santa. They also loved postcards, which were viewed as a fun and inexpensive way to advertise their wares.

Yes, right from the start, Santa was a hit, and his image became an increasingly familiar sight on printed material of all types. His figure on postcards, whether used to send messages to friends and family or to advertise a new product, was always a popular choice.

The 1863 portrait of Santa Claus found on this postcard is the work of American illustrator and caricaturist Thomas Nast. Influenced by Clement Clarke Moore's classic holiday poem, "A Visit From St. Nicholas," Nast is credited as the first artist to illustrate Santa Claus. Some of Nast's most famous drawings appeared in holiday issues of Harper's Weekly for over twenty years. They showed Santa decorating trees, making toys, going over his account books, and looking through his telescope for good children all over the world. The first suggestion that Santa lived at the North Pole came in 1882, when Nast drew Santa sitting on a box that was addressed: "Christmas Box 1882, St. Nicholas, North Pole."

HERE SANTA CLAUS AND MY GOOD WISHES REJOICE AT YOUR PROSPERITY,
MAY YOU BE HEALTHY, WISE AND WEALTHY, AND FREE FROM ALL ADVERSITY!

Louis Prang, an immigrant German lithographer, designed this Christmas postcard, which was printed
in the late 1880s. Prang is responsible for launching the greeting card industry in America.

Along with their use for holiday greetings, Santa postcards were used for the first time in the late 1800s for business correspondence and product promotion. In this postcard, notice that the typically Victorian gifts in Santa's pack are joined by boxes of Faulder's chocolates.

This rare 1894 postcard is used to advertise dolls, toys, and games from the Reuben Wood's Sons' Company, Syracuse, New York.

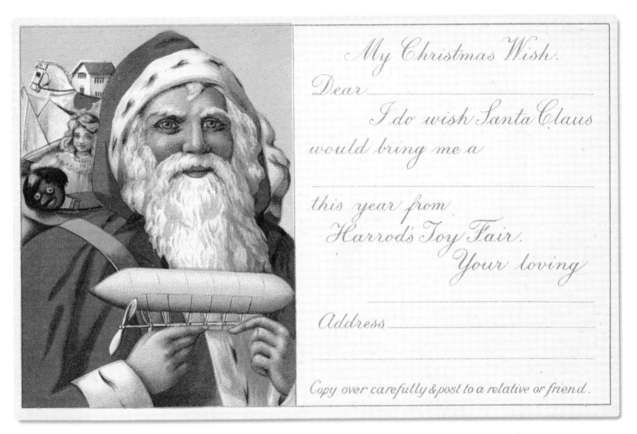

My Christmas Wish.

Dear _____

I do wish Santa Claus would bring me a _____

this year from Harrod's Toy Fair.

Your loving _____

Address _____

Copy over carefully & post to a relative or friend.

London's famous Harrod's department store used this postcard to promote its holiday toy fair. It provides a handy fill-in-the-blank shopping list for children to write out their gift requests before mailing the card to relatives and friends.

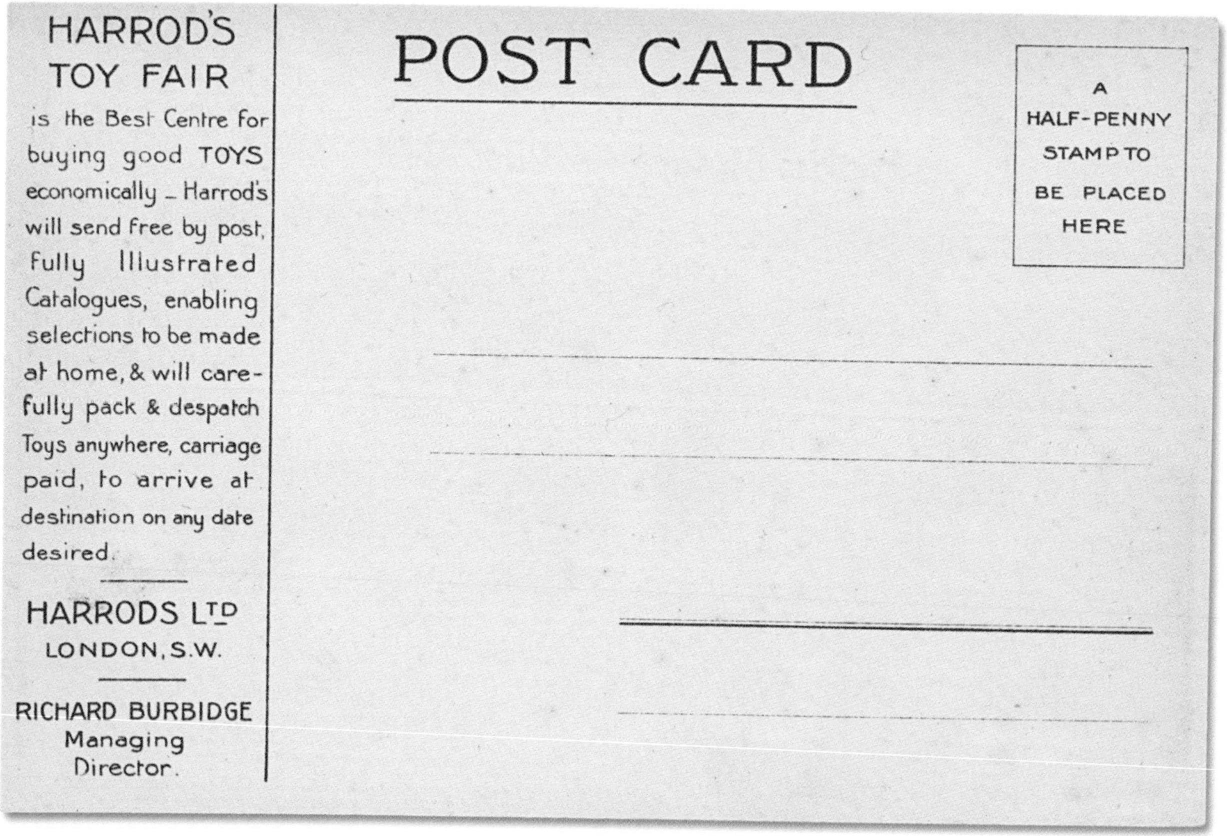

HARROD'S TOY FAIR

is the Best Centre for buying good TOYS economically — Harrod's will send free by post, fully Illustrated Catalogues, enabling selections to be made at home, & will carefully pack & despatch Toys anywhere, carriage paid, to arrive at destination on any date desired.

HARRODS LTD
LONDON, S.W.

RICHARD BURBIDGE
Managing
Director.

POST CARD

A
HALF-PENNY
STAMP TO
BE PLACED
HERE

A Visit From St. Nicholas

The most famous of all American Christmas poems, "The Night Before Christmas or an Account of a Visit From St. Nicholas" — most widely known as "A Visit From St. Nicholas" — first appeared anonymously in the Troy (New York) *Sentinel* on December 23, 1823. Gradually, as this poem grew in popularity, so did the question of its authorship. The issue remained unsettled until 1844 when Clement Clarke Moore, a professor of Greek Language and Literature at the New York Theological Seminary, included the poem in a collection of his writings. To many, he seemed a bit Puritan, and an unlikely author of Yuletide poetry, but among his friends, Moore was noted for his kindness and generosity.

According to holiday lore, Moore composed the poem in 1822 as a special Christmas gift for his two young daughters, Charity and Margaret. He began composing the happy couplets as he set out in his sleigh to buy a turkey for the upcoming holiday feast. Upon returning home, Moore consulted the writings of his friend Washington Irving, then combined his rhymes with Dutch legends to create "A Visit From St. Nicholas." Moore recited the poem for the first time to his daughters, and then repeated it for their Sunday school class. His wife then wrote it down in the family book, and an enthralled family friend submitted it to the *Sentinel* the following year. In 1837, a poetry anthology attributed the poem to Professor Moore, but it wasn't until 1844 that he acknowledged authorship.

Moore's authorship of the poem was challenged in 2000 by Professor Don Foster of Vassar College. Using "literary forensics"—an analysis of writing style aided by computer technology—Foster asserted that it was more likely that Major Henry Livingstone, who

The Night before Christmas

A Merry Christmas

lived from 1748 to 1828, had written the poem. For 150 years, Livingstone's heirs had claimed title to the work, and Foster's investigation strongly supported their contention. For instance, some of Livingstone's works written prior to 1823 included many of the same literary images found in "A Visit From St. Nicholas." Also, in his writings, Livingstone tended to use the word "all" as an adverb, overuse exclamation marks, and wish people a "Happy" rather than a "Merry" Christmas—all characteristics of the famous poem. Moreover, Foster discovered that Moore's collected poems included verses by his wife and some translated works by other poets. Although his research raised doubts about Moore's credibility, Foster is forced to admit that "nobody really knows" who wrote the Christmas poem. Three copies of "A Visit From St. Nicholas," autographed by Moore, exist, but there is no original manuscript by either claimant.

One thing, however, is certain. No matter who authored the famous holiday work, it has been and will continue to be a cherished part of the Christmas season for millions of families throughout America.

A Visit From St. Nicholas

Twas the night before Christmas,
  when all through the house
Not a creature was stirring,
  not even a mouse;
The stockings were hung
  by the chimney with care,
In hopes that St. Nicholas soon would be there.
The children were nestled all snug in their beds,
While visions of sugar-plums danced in their heads;

And mamma in her 'kerchief, and I in my cap,
Had just settled our brains for a long winter's nap,
When out on the lawn there arose such a clatter,
I sprang from the bed to see what was the matter.
Away to the window I flew like a flash,
Tore open the shutters and threw up the sash.

The moon on the breast of the new-fallen snow
Gave the lustre of mid-day to objects below,
When, what to my wondering eyes should appear
But a miniature sleigh, and eight tiny reindeer,

With a little old driver, so lively and quick,
I knew in a moment it must be St. Nick.

More rapid than eagles his coursers they came,
And he whistled, and shouted, and called them by name:
'Now, Dasher! now, Dancer! now, Prancer and Vixen!
On, Comet! on Cupid! on, Donder and Blitzen!
To the top of the porch! to the top of the wall!
Now dash away! dash away! dash away all!'

As dry leaves that before the wild hurricane fly,
When they meet with an obstacle, mount to the sky,
So up to the house-top the coursers they flew,
With the sleigh full of toys, and St. Nicholas too.
And then, in a twinkling, I heard on the roof
The prancing and pawing of each little hoof.

As I drew in my head, and was turning around,
Down the chimney St. Nicholas came with a bound.
He was dressed all in fur, from his head to his foot,
And his clothes were all tarnished with ashes and soot;

A bundle of toys he had flung on his back,
And he looked like a peddler just opening his pack.
His eyes — how they twinkled! his dimples how merry!
His cheeks were like roses, his nose like a cherry!
His droll little mouth was drawn up like a bow,
And the beard of his chin was as white as the snow;

The stump of a pipe he held tight in his teeth,
And the smoke it encircled his head like a wreath;

He had a broad face and a little round belly,
That shook when he laughed like a bowlful of jelly.
He was chubby and plump, a right jolly old elf,
And I laughed when I saw him, in spite of myself;
A wink of his eye and a twist of his head,
Soon gave me to know I had nothing to dread;

He spoke not a word, but went straight to his work,
And filled all the stockings; then turned with a jerk,
And laying his finger aside of his nose,
And giving a nod, up the chimney he rose;
He sprang to his sleigh, to his team gave a whistle,
And away they all flew like the down of a thistle.

But I heard him exclaim, ere he drove out of sight,

"Happy Christmas to all, and to all a good night."

—Clement Clarke Moore

Victorian trade card for department store D. McCarthy & Company beckons customers to visit its Santa Claus' Headquarters.

Products advertised on postcards and trade cards frequently featured Santa, often to the point of minimizing the actual product being promoted. This stunning Victorian card, featuring Santa with children in front of a beautifully decorated tree, is actually an advertisement for a box of wheat, which is barely noticeable on the table.

Santa has always been a natural salesman. This rather serious-looking Santa displays a hatbox full of toys from Stearns & Company department store in Cleveland, Ohio.

When Santa solicited great new "gotta-have" products, people believed their trusted friend.

Santa Claus

He comes in the night! He comes in the night!
   He softly, silently comes;
     While the little brown heads on the
       pillows so white
      Are dreaming of bugles and drums.
He cuts through the snow like a ship through the foam,
While the white flakes around him whirl;
Who tells him I know not, but he findeth
  the home
Of each good little boy and girl.

His sleigh it is long, and deep, and wide;
It will carry a host of things,
While dozens of drums hang over the side,
With the sticks sticking under the strings.
And yet not the sound of a drum is heard,
Not a bugle blast is blown,
As he mounts to the chimney-top like a bird,
And drops to the hearth like a stone.

The little red stockings he silently fills,
Till the stockings will hold no more;
The bright little sleds for the great snow hills
Are quickly set down on the floor.
Then Santa Claus mounts to the roof like a bird,
And glides to his seat in the sleigh;
     Not a sound of a bugle or drum is heard
     As he noiselessly gallops away.

    He rides to the West, and he rides to the East,
      Of his goodies he touches not one;
       He eateth the crumbs of the
        Christmas feast
When the dear little folks are done.
Old Santa Claus doeth all that he can;
This beautiful mission is his;
Then, children be good to the little old man,
When you find who the little man is.

—Author Unknown

This European postcard features Saint Nicholas as he prepares a sack of goodies to distribute on December 6, his feast day. This holiday is celebrated in German-speaking countries, Holland, and Belgium.

es, Virginia, There Is a Santa Claus

Eventually, most children question the existence of Santa Claus. One little girl not only posed this question to friends and family, but actually submitted it to a newspaper, thereby sparking an editorial that would be reprinted millions of times in newspapers all over the world.

Virginia O'Hanlon was eight years old in 1897, when schoolmates raised doubts that Santa Claus was real. It was a habit in her family to send their more perplexing questions to *The New York Sun,* her parents' favorite newspaper. So rather than directly answering his little girl's question, Virginia's father encouraged her to ask *The Sun* for "the real truth" about Santa.

Virginia's letter found its way into the hands of Francis P. Church, a veteran editor and the son of a Baptist minister. His reply would become one of the most famous in newspaper history:

We take pleasure in answering thus prominently the communication below, expressing at the same time our great gratification that its faithful author is numbered among the friends of The Sun:

Virginia, your little friends are wrong. They have been affected by the skepticism of a skeptical age. They do not believe except [what] they see. They think that nothing can be which is not comprehensible by their little minds. All minds, Virginia, whether they be men's or children's, are little. In this great universe of ours, man is a mere insect, an ant, in his intellect as compared with

Dear Editor—

I am 8 years old. Some of my little friends say there is no Santa Claus. Papa says, "If you see it in The Sun, it's so." Please tell me the truth, is there a Santa Claus?

Virginia O'Hanlon

the boundless world about him, as measured by the intelligence capable of grasping the whole of truth and knowledge.

Yes, Virginia, there is a Santa Claus. He exists as certainly as love and generosity and devotion exist, and you know that they abound and give to your life its highest beauty and joy. Alas! how dreary would be the world if there were no Santa Claus! It would be as dreary as if there were no Virginias. There would be no childlike faith then, no poetry, no romance to make tolerable this existence. We should have no enjoyment, except in sense and sight. The eternal light with which childhood fills the world would be extinguished.

* * * * *

No Santa Claus! Thank God! he lives, and he lives forever. A thousand years from now, Virginia, nay ten times ten thousand years from now, he will continue to make glad the heart of childhood.

The editorial was an instant sensation. It was translated into twenty languages, and *The Sun* reprinted it annually until the paper went out of business in 1949.

Virginia O'Hanlon went on to receive a Bachelor of Arts degree from Hunter College and a Master's from Columbia. In 1912, she began teaching in the New York City school system, and eventually, she became a principal. She married and had a daughter of her own. Throughout her life, Virginia received a steady stream of letters about her famous missive, and with each reply she included an attractive copy of the Frank Church editorial.

In 1971, at the age of eighty-one, Virginia O'Hanlon Douglas died in Valatie, New York. Frank Church had died years before, in 1906. But the message that Virginia O'Hanlon elicited from Frank Church lives on. In 1989, long after the death of both correspondents, someone pinned an unsigned Christmas card to the door of O'Hanlon's childhood home, along with a copy of Church's editorial. And even now, the phrase "Yes, Virginia, there is a Santa Claus" rings true to Santa lovers all over the world.

Dear Santa,

I am a little girl eight years old. I am at my Granmothers house, And I want a *something* braclet, pair, white boot and lot of candy, nut. And don't forget my sister she is six years old, and then there is my little brother he wants a train and that is all

Lovingly yours
judey

Children were often encouraged to write their holiday greetings on postcards, and then mail them to their young friends, cousins, or even Santa. As the little girl pictured on this card whispers a message to Santa, he appears to be selecting toys and dolls just for her.

A Merry Christmas.

During the holidays, postcards featuring figures of Christmas gift givers were mailed back and forth across the sea in great numbers.

A bright and happy Christmas

CHAPTER TWO

Santa Comes of Age 1900–1919

During the early years of the new century, most of the world was at peace. In America, it was an exciting time to be alive. The country was enjoying a period of prosperity—one filled with exciting new inventions and abundant employment opportunities. Immigration was at an all-time high. And Santa was fit and happy.

The period from 1908 to 1917 is considered the Golden Age of Postcards. With postage at a penny (and only slightly more for some overseas mailings), postcards were fashionable, inexpensive, and enormously popular. They had become the most widely used form of communication and were issued for all occasions. It is estimated that over 100 million postcards were printed and mailed during this nine-year period, providing a unique look into turn-of-the-century life, art, and celebrations. Many thousands of these cards with images of Santa Claus still exist and are found in private collections and museums all over the world.

At Christmas, as in the period before the turn of the century, families new to America continued sending holiday postcards back home and received them in return. People were homesick at Christmas, and these images were warm and friendly reminders of the places they had left behind. Correspondence with family and friends was so important, and quick postcard messages were both fun to write and easy to send.

At the beginning of the twentieth century, Christmas had become our most popular holiday. Americans everywhere decorated trees, exchanged presents, and sent postcards bearing greetings of the season. When Santa appeared on these greeting-type cards, not only was he shown riding in his sleigh, making toys, or checking gift lists, he was also pictured doing lots of trendy things that were fashionable and exciting. He flew planes, talked on telephones, and drove cars.

The popular Art Nouveau movement, with its characteristic flowing lines and graceful, sinuous curves, influenced many cards of this period, and illustrations of Santa incorporated many design elements of this artistic style. It was also a time when original hand-drawn Santa postcards were beginning to appear. Amateur or professional, people began creating their own illustrations on cards along with personal messages of the season.

Retailers continued to use postcards to advertise products or services, and they counted on Santa's trustworthy image to help. The ads themselves may have appeared on the cards, but it was that warm and wonderful Santa on the front that did the real talking. The adage "a picture is worth a thousand words" certainly rang true. It was the first time that Santa began to emerge as the early "selling czar of Madison Avenue," and from this point on, his endorsements would know no bounds. In addition to endorsing products, Santa began backing political and social causes for the first time. He appeared on postcards that supported issues such as "Votes for Woman" and promoted organizations like the American Red Cross. Because of his affiliation, these cards were widely circulated and typically received special notice. Even Mrs. Claus got into the act in 1908, when well-known storyteller Georgene Faulkner presented herself as Santa's wife and entranced children with her readings of holiday stories.

Initially, outstanding printing techniques made Germany the premier producer of postcards. England and the United States had printers of their own, but their cards did not compare with the German product. This changed, however, with the onset of World War I. Trade restrictions and sanctions prohibited imports from Germany, and American printers and publishers took the postcard lead. It didn't take long to find Santa on war postcards, and his appeal was universal. Everyone claimed him. During the war years, Santa's look reflected the strain of conflict. Often pictured promoting the war effort, Santa was thinner and less jovial than he had been in the past. But although his image was more sober and restrained, Santa never failed to offer support, good cheer, and the promise of better times.

At Christmas, as in the period before the turn of the century, families new to America continued
sending postcards back home and received them in return.

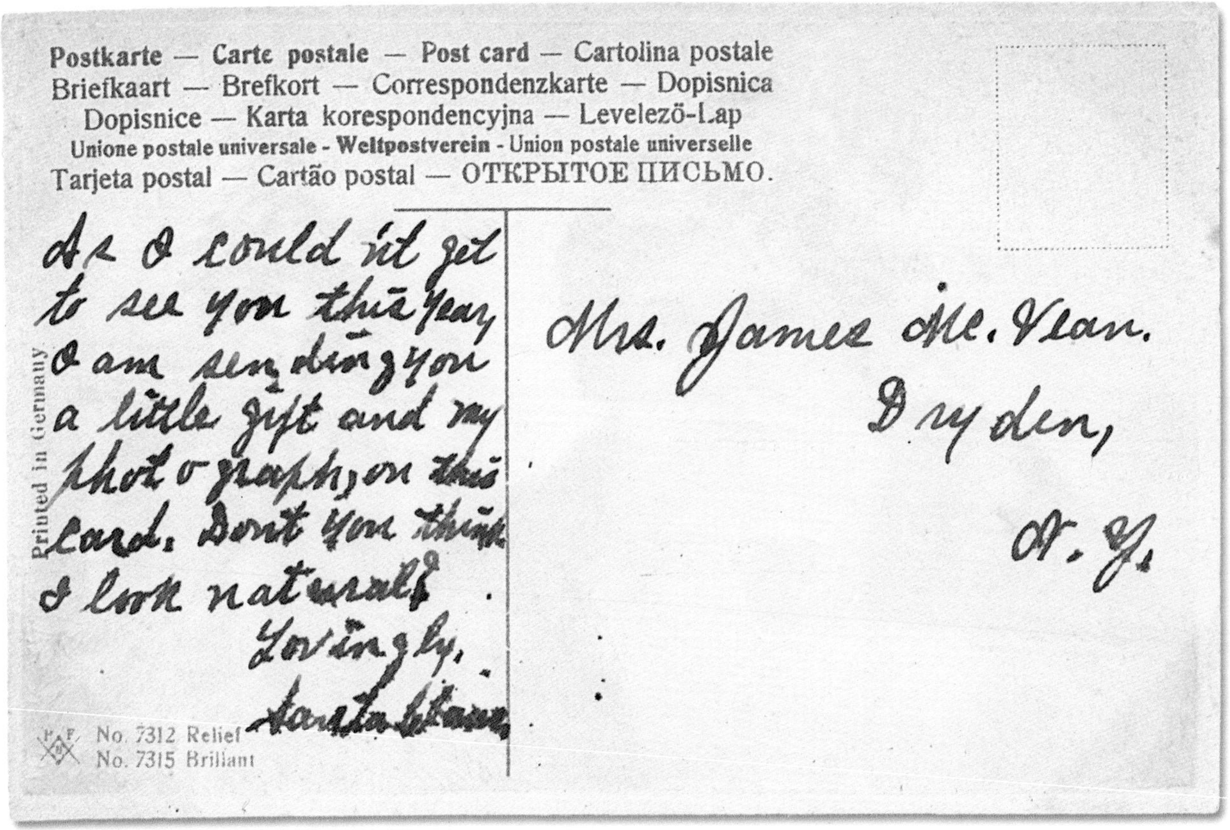

Postkarte — Carte postale — Post card — Cartolina postale
Briefkaart — Brefkort — Correspondenzkarte — Dopisnica
Dopisnice — Karta korespondencyjna — Levelező-Lap
Unione postale universale - Weltpostverein - Union postale universelle
Tarjeta postal — Cartão postal — ОТКРЫТОЕ ПИСЬМО.

As I could'nt get
to see you this year
I am sending you
a little gift and my
photograph on this
card. Don't you think
I look natural?
        Lovingly,
            Santa Claus

Printed in Germany

P.F. No. 7312 Relief
No. 7315 Brilliant

Mrs. James Mc. Lean.
        Dryden,
            N. Y.

MERRY CHRISTMAS.

These turn-of-the-century holiday cards show a playful Santa peeking out from behind a curtain, much to the delight of children.

These Tuck's Post Cards are samples of the many holiday cards produced by English-based Raphael Tuck & Sons, deemed "ART PUBLISHERS TO THEIR MAJESTIES THE KING & QUEEN."

A LETTER FROM SANTA CLAUS

My Dear Son

I hope this letter finds you well. Father and I are as well as can be expected. We look forward to your visit in the Spring and are counting the days until we get to see our new grandson.

Love,

Mother

The front of this postcard includes a miniature envelope, containing a small piece of paper with a personal message [c. 1910].

Post Card

THIS SIDE FOR THE ADDRESS.

My Dear Son I thank you for your morning note it is very nice of course I wear it every morning Joseph is my comrade you see I am doing as I think as you know boys will know send you something dear Mother

Mr James M. Beam
Fifth St
Bay side
N.Y.

DEC 31 7-PM 1910

Postcards often reflected the nation's different areas of progress. The cards at left illustrate the advent of the wireless communication system and the historic completion of the Panama Canal.

Images of holiday gift givers from many countries graced the fronts of postcards. Renderings of an American Santa Claus and a French Père Noël appear on these early twentieth-century cards.

A Merry Christmas

9007

Joyeux Noël!

Good Saint Nicholas

Americans love and cherish Santa Claus, but long before his appearance in the nineteenth century, the tradition of giving with a joyous heart was identified with Saint Nicholas—a real person who lived around 300 AD. An advocate of Christianity, Nicholas became the youngest bishop in the history of the Church when he assumed control of the diocese of Myra on the southern coast of Turkey. Once the site of a temple to Apollo, which had been destroyed by an earthquake, the place where Nicholas lived is a twentieth-century tourist attraction.

Nicholas was revered as a devout bishop who was most esteemed for personal acts of charity, which he performed under the cover of darkness. He gave away most of his wealth in the form of gifts to the needy, especially children. According to legend, Nicholas' most famous act was rescuing the three daughters of an impoverished nobleman from being sold into slavery. He helped the girls by tossing three bags of gold for their dowries through an open window of their home. His frequent acts of generosity made him the patron saint of maidens. After Nicholas died, his burial place at Myra became a shrine that was visited by countless petitioners from all Europe. Eventually, he was elevated to sainthood.

Gradually, followers of Saint Nicholas spread throughout Europe. As early as the sixth century, Emperor Justinian dedicated a church in his honor in Constantinople. It was the first of hundreds of churches across the continent that would bear Nicholas' name. Interestingly, he had more churches named in his honor than any of Jesus' disciples. Even more impressive, Nicholas became the patron saint of both Greece and Russia. Further proof of his continuing prominence came late in the eleventh century when his bones were kidnapped from Myra by Italian merchants and moved to a basilica in Bari, Italy. That church then became a popular pilgrimage destination.

By the twelfth century, every December 6—the feast day of Saint Nicholas—it was customary for Europeans to exchange small gifts. This day marked the inaugural event of each Christmas season, and every anonymous gift was attributed to the intervention of this beloved saint. The popularity of Saint Nicholas continued through the years. When Columbus made landfall in Haiti on December 6, 1492, he named the welcoming bay Puerto de San Nicolas in honor of Europe's favorite saint. During the Renaissance, sailors (including pirates), thieves, and moneychangers were added to the list of those who believed that Saint Nicholas provided them a voice in heaven.

But Nicholas has not fared as well in modern times. As a result of the Protestant Reformation, he lost his prominent spot in most countries as the legendary gift-giving Christmas icon, and was replaced by less religious figures. In the United States, Saint Nicholas was the precursor to Santa Claus, who first appeared during the nineteenth century. In 1969, the Catholic Church, admitting the lack of evidence surrounding his life, removed Nicholas' name from its Calendar of Saints. Nevertheless, his hold on the minds of people around the world still exists, and his name continues to be invoked by countless numbers of devotees. Americans would never have envisioned Santa Claus had it not been for his influence.

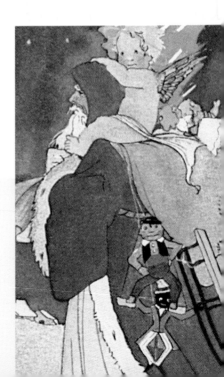

A little French girl dreams of the famous Cirque d'Hiver (Winter Circus), while Père Noël leaves her gifts of toy clowns and circus animals, making her dream come true.

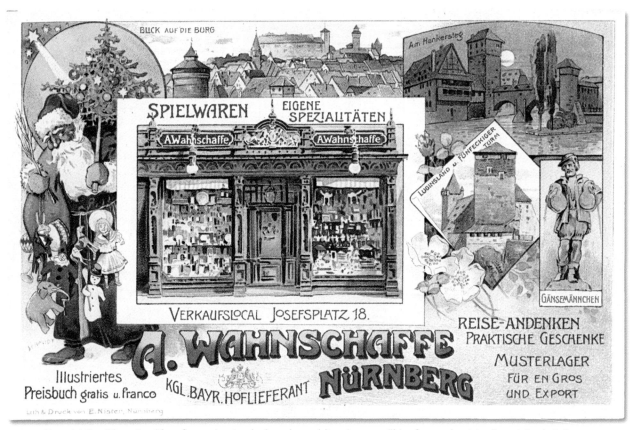

Every detail on this postcard for a German toy store is shown in exquisite color, exemplifying Germany's outstanding printing techniques.

Retailers continually found ways to associate their products with Santa's trustworthy image. This 1909 postcard from the Rockford Watch Company was designed by R.F. Outcault, the creator of the famous Yellow Kid comic-strip character and the Buster Brown shoe advertisements.

Gatchel & Manning
the
Designers & Engravers
of Philadelphia

wish you
and yours
the Season's
Greetings

1911

1910

Philadelphia engravers Gatchel & Manning used Santa on this 1910 postcard to send consumers best wishes for the New Year.

Children who sent letters to Santa via the Children's Editor of the *Baltimore News* received this postcard in return. The back of the card, shown on page 46, has a personal note from Santa himself.

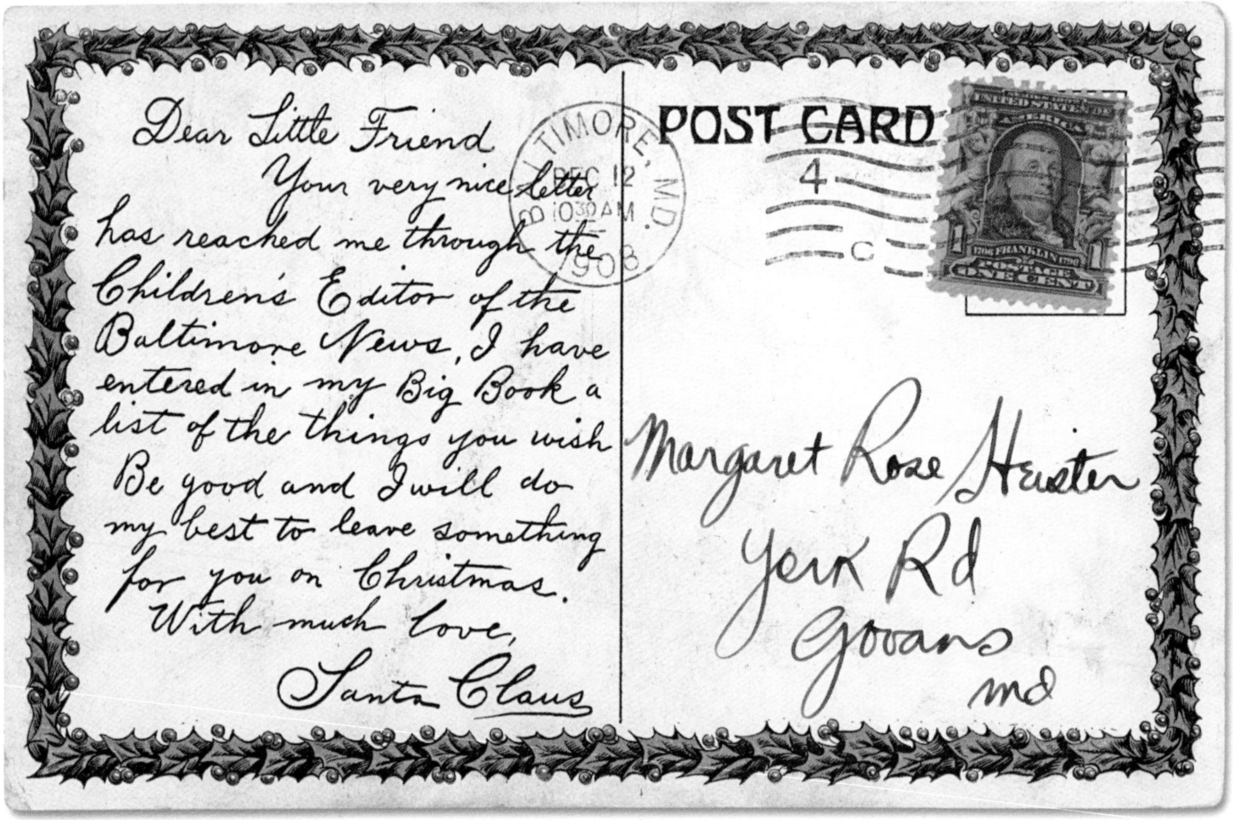

Dear Little Friend

Your very nice letter has reached me through the Children's Editor of the Baltimore News. I have entered in my Big Book a list of the things you wish. Be good and I will do my best to leave something for you on Christmas.

With much love,

Santa Claus

POST CARD

BALTIMORE, MD.
DEC 12
10:30 AM
1908

4
C

UNITED STATES OF AMERICA
1706 FRANKLIN 1790
POSTAGE ONE CENT

Margaret Rose Heuster
York Rd
Govans
md

Dear Sir,

In sending you our annual XMAS GREETING FROM THE LAND OF TOYS AND DOLLS we wish to thank you for your liberal patronage and to assure you, that we appreciate the same.

We hope by carefully studying the markets to be able to offer you a better line of goods in 1907 than ever before and trust, that we may have the privelege of showing you this line and booking your order,

Office of
SIBLEY,
LINDSAY
& CURR Cº
Chemnitz.
Germany.

FRÖHLICHE WEIHNACHTEN

Yours truly
SIBLEY, LINDSAY & CURR Co.
per W. J. Harkness, Buyer.

This 1907 postcard from the German office of Sibley, Lindsay & Curr department store, sends its Christmas "greeting from the land of toys and dolls."

Leather postcards, such as this one sent from Pahloren, Illinois, enjoyed a popular although brief period of use. The problem? Stamps often fell off during transit.

Meet me Face to Face at BISCHOF'S CO-OPERATIVE BIG STORE
CRAWFORDSVILLE, INDIANA

Macy's—the biggest department store in the world—started a holiday tradition when it hired the first real Santa Claus to listen to children's Christmas wishes. Many department stores throughout the country quickly began to follow suit. The real-life Santa pictured in this 1908 postcard invites customers to meet him at a store in Crawfordsville, Indiana.

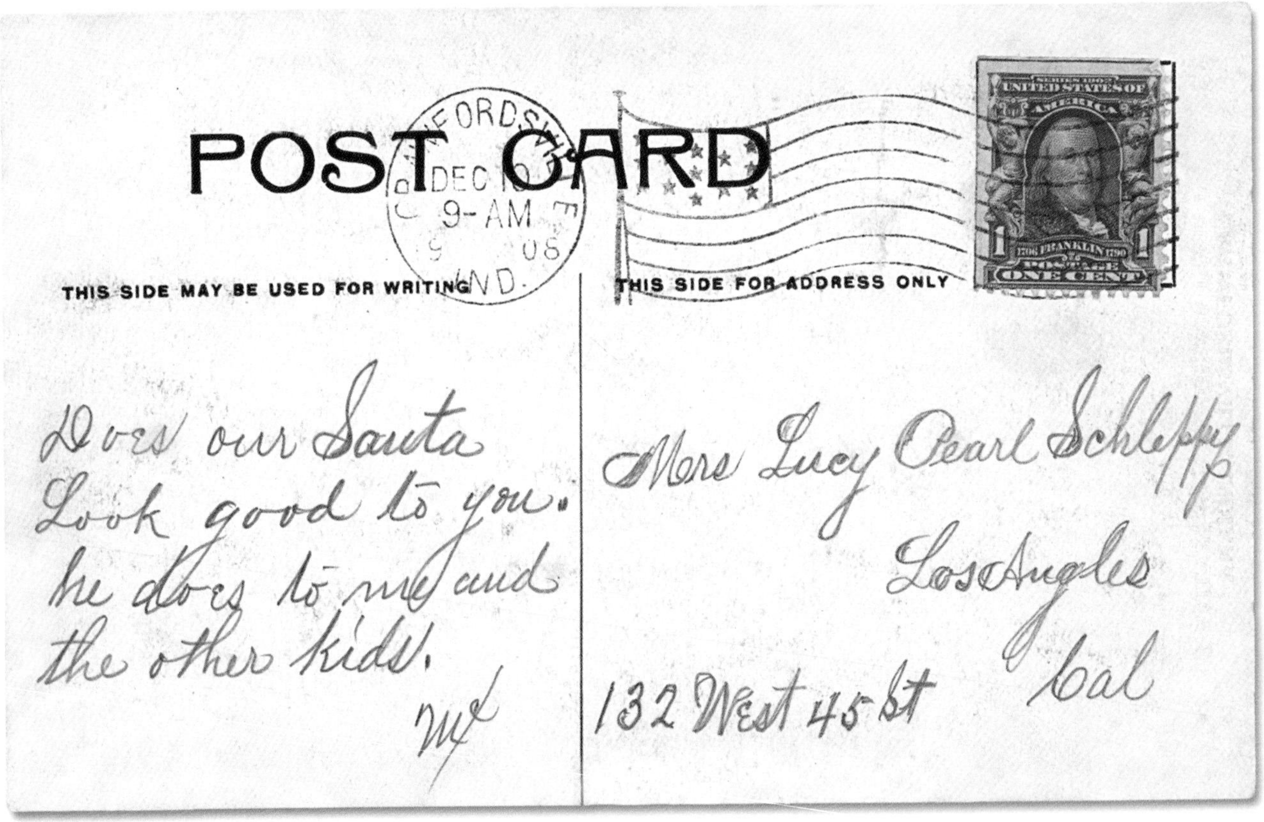

POST CARD

THIS SIDE MAY BE USED FOR WRITING | THIS SIDE FOR ADDRESS ONLY

Does our Santa
Look good to you.
he does to me and
the other kids.
mx

Mrs Lucy Pearl Schleppy

Los Angles

132 West 45 St

Cal

CHRISTMAS GREETINGS FROM IDAHO FALLS, IDAHO.

No. 61

MOONLIGHT ON THE BEAUTIFUL SNAKE RIVER

Santa was often added to Christmas greetings on postcards from towns and cities. These cards typically displayed inset photos of restaurants parks, hotels, or interesting landmarks of the area.

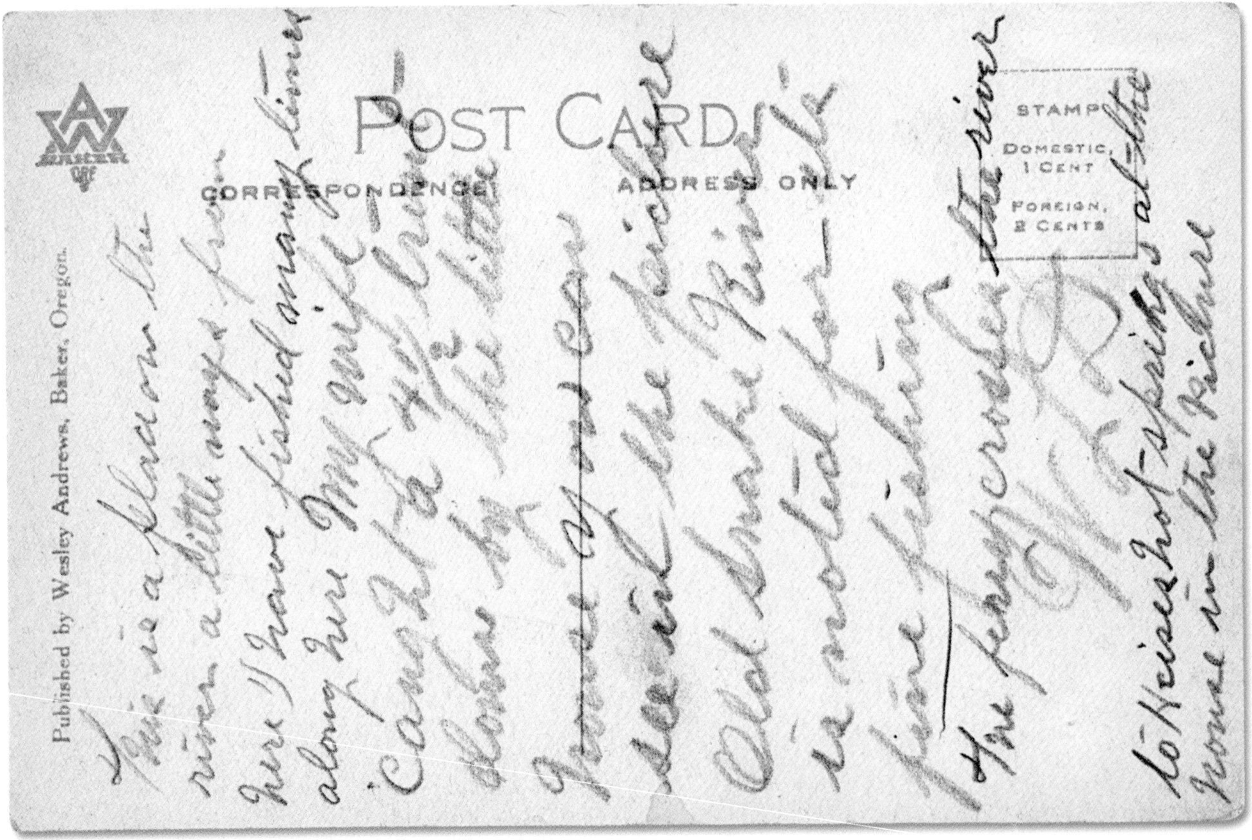

Published by Wesley Andrews, Baker, Oregon.

POST CARD

CORRESPONDENCE

ADDRESS ONLY

STAMP
DOMESTIC, 1 CENT
FOREIGN, 2 CENTS

This is a place on the
river a little ways from
here I have fished many times
along here My wife
caught a 40 lb trout
down by the little
~~house you can~~
see in the picture
Old Snake River
is noted for its
fine fishing
The ferry crosses the river
to Heise hot springs at the
house in the picture

A Merry Christmas

From Des Moines, Iowa

When Santa Claus Comes

good time is coming, I wish it were here,
The very best time in the whole of the year;
I'm counting each day on my fingers
   and thumbs —
the weeks that must pass before Santa Claus comes.

Then when the first snowflakes begin to come down,
And the wind whistles sharp and the branches
  are brown,
I'll not mind the cold, though my fingers it numbs,
For it brings the time nearer when Santa Claus comes.

—Author Unknown

Santa's kind face graces the front of this postcard created especially for "sweethearts."

"I'm coming little boys & girls. With lots of pretty playthings"—

1906-4"

The Arts and Crafts Movement, which began in England in the 1860s and filtered to the United States around the turn of the century, evolved as a reaction to the Industrial Revolution. In a world that was turning toward mass-produced factory-made items, followers of the movement strove to preserve the craftsmanship of hand manufacturing in such areas as boot making, bookbinding, and furniture making. A reflection of the Arts and Crafts Movement was perhaps also seen in the many hand-made postcards created in the early 1900s.

Along with professionally printed cards, many amateur artists tried their hand at creating holiday cards of their own, as seen in this 1906 example.

Hark! The Christmas Bells are ringing,
  And the Heavenly choir is singing,
Let us pause and rest a moment
  In this happy atmosphere.
Let us leave our bales of sorrow
  With the past, and face the morrow
With a stack of smile begetters
  That will last through out the year.
                    —— E.R. Bailey.
Christmas 1913

E.R.Bailey-13-

The creator of this 1913 hand-drawn postcard composed a holiday poem to go along with the original drawing of Santa.

Merry Christmas Miss Bunting from Frances Johnson

Santa looks very much like a portly Victorian gentleman in this cheery hand-made postcard from the early 1900s.

A cleverly drawn postcard finds Santa riding high atop a holly-leaf sleigh.

At the beginning of the twentieth century, most illustrators did not incorporate religious and secular elements on the same card.
In this unusual 1909 postcard, Santa pushes the Baby Jesus in a sled.

Merry Christmas Around the World

CHINESE   *Shung Dán Kwailéh*

DANISH   *Alvorlig Jul*

FINNISH   *Iloinen Joulu*

FRENCH   *Joyeux Noël*

GERMAN   *Frohe Weihnachten*

HAWAIIAN   *Mele Kalikimaka*

ITALIAN   *Buon Natale*

JAPANESE   *Mari Karisamasu*

POLISH   *Wesoy Boze Narodzenie*

PORTUGUESE *Alegre Natal*

SPANISH   *Feliz Navidad*

SWEDISH   *Glad Jul*

Postcards often depicted Santa engaged in popular or trendy activities. This silk-embossed 1910 card has him delivering presents by automobile.

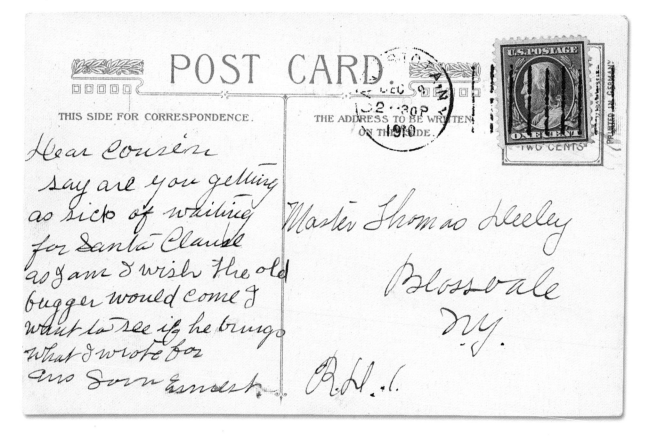

POST CARD.

THIS SIDE FOR CORRESPONDENCE.

THE ADDRESS TO BE WRITTEN
ON THIS SIDE.

Dear Cousin
    say are you getting
as sick of waiting
for Santa Claus
as I am I wish the old
bugger would come I
want to see if he brings
what I wrote for
ans Soon Ernest

Master Thomas Sleeley

Blossvale

N.Y.

R.H.1.

Santa the salesman flies in a "typewriter" airplane with a message to parents: "Your boy, your girl should have a 1911 Simplex Typewriter."

Gimme a Little Kiss

Getting a kiss while standing under a sprig of mistletoe is one of the holiday's most endearing customs. According to the tradition, one of the plant's berries must be plucked off after each kiss. When the berries are gone, there is to be no more kissing! This symbol of romance, which represents peace, happiness, and good luck, is believed to have its origins in the Scandinavian myth of Balder, the Norse god of the sun.

It seems that Frigga, Balder's mother and goddess of love, sought promises from air, fire, water, earth, and all of the plants and animals never to hurt her son. But Frigga forgot about the mistletoe plant, which grew neither on nor under the earth, but on apple and oak trees. Loki, the evil enemy of Balder, was determined to kill him. He tricked his blind brother, Hodor, into throwing a spear tipped with mistletoe at Balder, killing him.

The death of Balder meant the death of the sun, and soon a bleak, cold winter darkened the world. Without sunlight, plants withered and animals died. Brokenhearted over her son's death, Frigga cried tears that dropped onto the mistletoe and turned into the plant's white berries. The gods, aware that the world needed sunlight, restored Balder to life. Ecstatic, Frigga stood under the mistletoe and declared that the plant must bring love, not death, into the world. She planted grateful kisses on anyone who passed under it.

CHRISTMAS GREETINGS

The popular Art Nouveau movement, characterized by flowing lines and graceful, sinuous curves, influenced many postcards of this period. The cards at left incorporate many design elements of this artistic style.

Santa, complete with an overflowing sack of toys, offered warm and cheery holiday grettings on many postcards of the period.

WHEN YOU'RE ASLEEP ON CHRISTMAS EVE,
MAY SANTA CLAUS COME ROUND AND LEAVE
A HOST OF LOVELY SWEETS AND TOYS,
FOR YOU AND ALL THE GIRLS AND BOYS!
MAY BYRON

The Seasons Greetings and Best Wishes

%o Hazel

from

Aunt Grace

In the early 1900s, in addition to endorsing products, Santa began promoting organizations for the first time.
Santa Claus and Father Time extend year-end greetings in this 1909 postcard from the American Red Cross.

E. M. Harmon

Santa even had a hand in backing political movements. In this 1917 postcard, he supports the women's right to vote.

"Merry Christmas."

Georgene Faulkner
as
"Mrs. Santa Claus"

Story Telling for Children
SPECIAL PROGRAMS

The character of Mrs. Claus had always been pictured as a happy homemaker who spent most of her time cooking meals, mending elves' clothing, and making dear old Santa comfortable. In 1908, she took on a new role when Chicago's famous "Story Lady," Georgene Faulkner, presented herself as Santa's wife. As Mrs. Claus, she captivated the hearts and minds of children everywhere with her repertoire of enchanting holiday tales.

When World War I broke out, it didn't take long to find Santa on postcards that reflected the conflict, and every country claimed him as theirs. With such universal appeal, Santa took no sides, and graced the cards of many different nations. In general, however, Santa's look reflected the strain of war. Not quite as joyful as he had been pictured in the past, Santa was a more serious figure whose primary job was to support the war effort by upholding the hopes of the nation.

Old Nick's here
with greetings to you
While we're raising Nick with the Huns

For Y.M.C.A.   Devambez Paris.

In this unique World War I postcard, Santa has traded his red suit for a military uniform. With a pack of American doughboys on his back, he crosses the Atlantic in pursuit of a German soldier.

Santa's Coming

Old Santa must be coming,
Fast speeding on his way!
Don't you hear the tramp of reindeer,
And the bells upon his sleigh?
And a jolly pack of gifts he'll leave
For a Merry Christmas day!

—Author Unknown

In a patriotic gesture, a World War I Belgian soldier passes out his country's flag while being carried in Santa's gift sack.

A small Santa is found in the lettering at the top of this World War I card, in which a little girl teaches an American soldier French from her textbook.

A MERRY CHRISTMAS
AND A HAPPY NEW YEAR FROM
THE AMERICAN PEOPLE THROUGH
THE AMERICAN RED CROSS

Postcards during World War I that displayed holiday gift giving were popular. In the card on the far left, an American GI offers Christmas presents to a little French girl, while the card at right shows a uniformed Santa whose arms are filled with presents for wounded soldiers.

THE CHRISTMAS SHIP, America's Messenger to the War-Made Orphans Across the Sea

U. S. COLLIER JASON

THE FLAG OF PEACE ★ "INASMUCH"

SPEED AWAY. SPEED AWAY. ON THY ERRAND OF LIGHT.
MAKING FOR CHILDREN A CHRISTMAS BRIGHT.

Flying under the flag of peace, Santa's Christmas ship, the U.S. *Collier Jason*, was "America's messenger to the war-made orphans across the sea."

CHAPTER THREE

Santa Between the Wars 1920–1940

It was the beginning of a new decade. The "war to end all wars" was over, our soldiers were back home, and the mood of the country was upbeat. The Roaring Twenties appropriately described a nation that was alive with flappers and the Charleston, as well as bootlegged whiskey and speakeasies. Jazz and swing music filled the air. Americans everywhere enjoyed their new personal freedoms. People began traveling again, and visits abroad were encouraged. However, the country's merriment came to a halt with the stock market crash in 1929, after which a sobering ten-year period known as the Great Depression took over. Throughout these two decades, Santa was right in the thick of things—through the good times and the bad, the prosperity and the poverty.

Postcards from the early 1920s typically pictured a plump, happy postwar Santa dancing or singing. He had a grand old time celebrating "better times are here again." Airplanes, automobiles, and baseball had captivated America's attention, and Santa enjoyed them, too. Many famous artists of the day, includ-ing Ellen Clapsaddle, Rose O'Neill, Bernhardt Wall, and Francis Brundage, designed postcards that depicted Santa fishing, skiing, swimming, and even sleeping (thank you, Norman Rockwell).

Once more, we find Santa marketing products and encouraging commercialism. Unfortunately, only a few good years would pass before the stock market crashed, ushering in a period of great hardship. It was a time when economic despair gripped the nation. Conditions went from wanting nothing to needing everything. Never had so many men been out of work. Families were barely surviving, and the prospects for improvement were dim. Santa also suffered. Illustrators were quick to grasp the new mood, and Santa's appearance began to change, reflecting the downward turn. Although he still had a smile on his face, Santa was not quite as jolly as he had been in less stressful times, and he was rarely pictured laden with gifts.

Given a pause in his selling career, Santa was soon called upon by the government to act as a motivator for the county. He served as a reminder to Americans that although life was diffi-cult, good times were sure to come again. As President Wood-row Wilson had done during World War I, President Calvin Coolidge used Santa's popularity to help calm the fears of strug-gling Americans. Inspirational messages on postcards com-monly accompanied Santa and his endorsements. Eventually, President Franklin D. Roosevelt would use him as a partner in creating the Works Progress Administration (WPA). And during World War II, Santa would assist Roosevelt by promoting the sale of war bonds and stamps. By comparison, European Santas were illustrated differently. The overseas Santa often appeared thin and haggard, even scary looking.

During this period, photographs were often used on post-card fronts. On many holiday photo cards, children were posed with Santa. During the Depression, when children had so little, taking a photo with this favorite Christmas figure was consid-ered a special treat. Children's messages to Santa, which humbly asked him to leave pieces of candy or fruit in their Christmas stockings, or pairs of warm socks under the tree, were further reflections of the impoverished times.

When Prohibition ended in the early 1930s, Santa's counte-nance soon appeared on ads that supported beer and liquor sales, as well as cigarettes and cigars. And he continued endors-ing these products for many years. It wouldn't be until the end of the century that advertisements for tobacco and alcohol would face government restrictions. Only then would Santa be liberated from his selling duty.

It was also during the 1930s that illustrator Haddon Sundblom introduced a new and improved Santa to the world. In the first of a long line of ads for the Coca-Cola Company, Sundblom presented a realistic-looking round-faced rosy-cheeked Santa, who became the model for future Santas, including the one we know and love today.

At the end of the 1930s, Europe was at war and the United States was on the brink of involvement. The world was positioned for conflict. Lines were drawn, but universally beloved, Santa as-sumed his role in the war effort on both sides of the Atlantic.

A Merry Christmas

You're in my Christmas circuit
And on the waves of thought
A Happy Christmas and New Year
To you is gladly brought.

Bringing You
"A MERRY CHRISTMAS"
While driving in his auto-sleigh
He laughs at speeding-laws,
For his license is provided
With a special Santa clause.

512

The early years of the 1920s saw postcards that typically pictured a plump, happy postwar Santa. The cards often included images and verse that cleverly reflected the popular advancements of the time, such as the radio and automobile.

The Christmas Gift
From the Sea

To Harry Alexander
From Miss Jeanette Alexander

COPYRIGHT 1921, BY FRANK E. DAVIS FISH CO.

Santa overlooks the day's catch on this 1921 postcard from the Frank E. Davis Fish Company.

"Real photo" postcards were very popular during the 1920s and 1930s. On holiday cards, children posing with Santa was common. Typically, these cards were created in a photo studio or department store, where children were placed on a set with Santa. Especially during the Depression, when children had so little, taking a photo with this favorite Christmas figure was considered a holiday highlight.

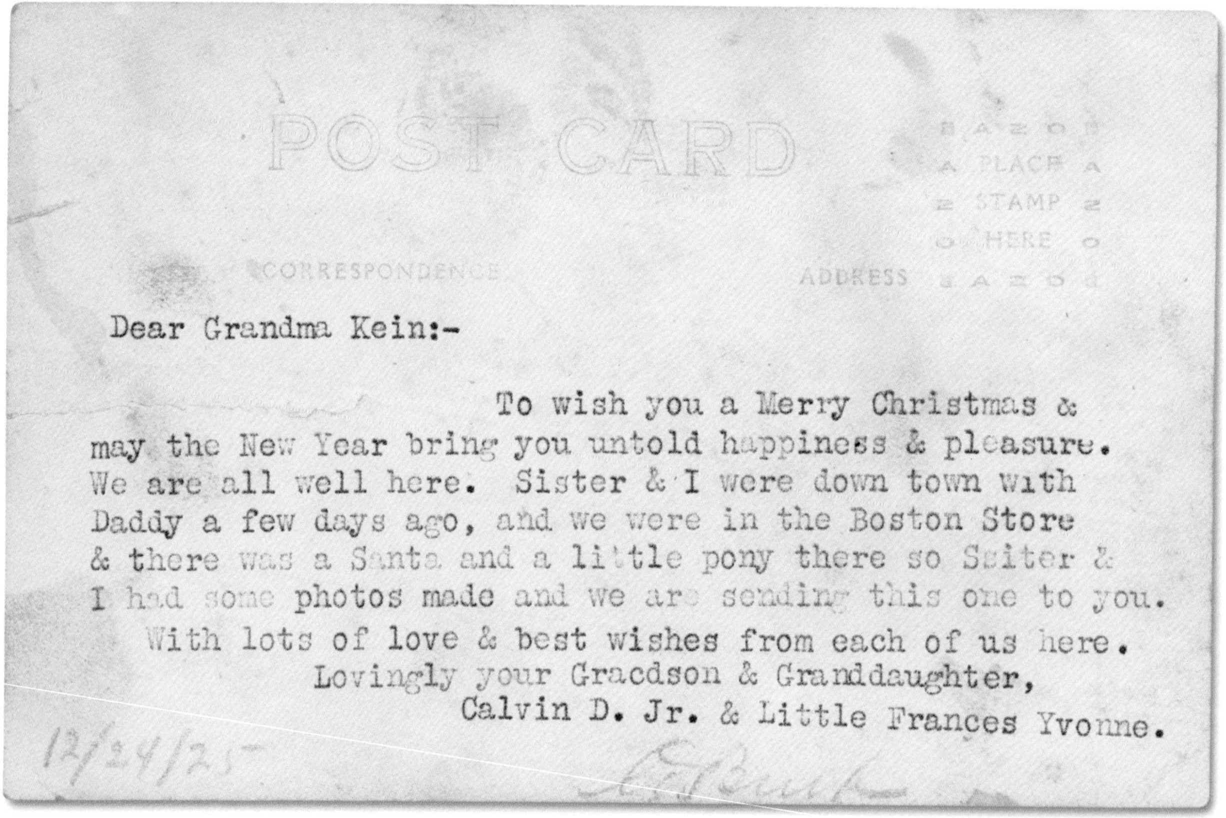

POST CARD

CORRESPONDENCE

A PLACE A
STAMP
HERE

ADDRESS

Dear Grandma Kein:-

To wish you a Merry Christmas &
may the New Year bring you untold happiness & pleasure.
We are all well here. Sister & I were down town with
Daddy a few days ago, and we were in the Boston Store
& there was a Santa and a little pony there so Ssiter &
I had some photos made and we are sending this one to you.
With lots of love & best wishes from each of us here.
Lovingly your Graedson & Granddaughter,
Calvin D. Jr. & Little Frances Yvonne.

12/24/25

This late 1920s postcard of a sleigh ride with Santa is a treasured memento.

Santa and one of his friends are pictured flying on the North Pole Express in this "real photo" postcard.

MERRY CHRISTMAS!
I'm sure my wishes
will come true,
'Cause Santa's taking
them to you.

AT CHRISTMAS
This jolly little card
I send
With jolly wishes
for a friend.

A decorative parade
of toys borders
each of these jolly
images of Santa.

mes chers Petits amis.
me voici comme tous les ans revenu au
Bon marché à Bruxelles. Je vous y attends en
compagnie de vos Parents et me fais une joie
de vous offrir une gentille surprise
S.t Nicolas

Wearing his bishop's robe and hat, Saint Nicholas drops gifts down a chimney in this 1922 postcard from Belgium.

Christmas in Europe

Christmas marks the birth of Christ, the child Jesus whose life is the core of the Christian faith. But the Bible offers no clues as to the actual date of his Nativity, and one of the achievements of the early Church was to choose a birthday acceptable to all. Long before the time of Christ, the winter solstice—the shortest day of the year, signifying a reversal of the death of the sun—was celebrated by many cultures. And within the Roman Empire, the end of each December featured Saturnalia, a week of jubilation to welcome the new year. After the advent of Christianity, Church leaders wisely took advantage of the existing season of joy, and Pope Liberius authorized the celebration of Christmas on December 25.

Europe has more successfully maintained the religious aspects of Christmas than the United States. On the Continent, celebrations of Christ's birth have traditionally been separated from purely gift-giving occasions. In Europe, depending on the location, the exchange of presents could come as soon as Saint Nicholas' feast day, or as late as early January with the Feast of the Epiphany, also called "Little Christmas." Attendance at a religious service on Christmas Day is very important in Europe—more so than it is across the Atlantic. Yet by no means does this more solemn aspect hinder the celebration of the season.

Europe has provided Americans with many of their most cherished Christmas traditions. Reverence for the evergreen tree came out of Germany, Scandinavians burn the Yule log and tell legends of a man named Kris Kringle, Saint Nicholas came to America via the Dutch settlers of New Amsterdam, and no Christmas season would be complete without a performance of Tchaikovsky's *The Nutcracker* or a viewing of Charles Dickens' *A Christmas Carol.* Even the exchange of Christmas cards began in Europe.

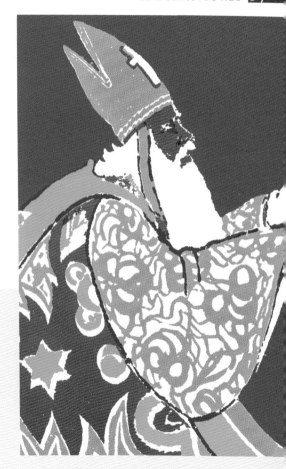

Many other European celebrations remain unique. For example, Saint Nicholas still brings gifts to Dutch children with the aid of *Zwarte Piet* (Black Pete), his Moorish servant. Pete, who may have originally been black because of ashes from chimneys, is responsible for throwing sweets into the wooden shoes of good children. In Russia, Grandfather Frost traditionally delivered Christmas gifts, but his identification with outmoded religious thinking made him an unacceptable figure to Communists. In the 1920s, Stalin himself approved the New Year's Day exchange of presents from Ded Moroz, a thin and imperious gentleman who drives a troika and is often accompanied by the Snow Princess. Less than 15 percent of Russians celebrate Christmas on December 25, but millions more exchange gifts on New Year's or on the Orthodox Christmas Day in early January. Across Scandinavia, a Santa-like figure called Jultomten brings joy and gifts to believing children. In Sweden, traditionally, the eldest daughter serves her parents cake and coffee in bed on Christmas Day while wearing a halo of candles. And in England, Santa has competition from a rather gaunt Father Christmas, who wears a brown hooded garment and is crowned with sprigs of holly.

In France, children, who once awaited the visit of Père Noël by placing their shoes at a hearth, now put more trust in their parents and Santa Claus. French cats eat extremely well, for a year's bad luck follows if they mew on Christmas. Traditionally, Armenians eat a lot of spinach on Christmas Day, Poles enjoy a special wafer bread, and Belgians celebrate with mussels.

In the more Latin areas of Europe, including Portugal, Spain, and Italy, Christmas traditions often include a menu of assorted fish for the Christmas Eve feast, while attendance at Midnight Mass is another accepted part of the celebration. After the completion of *Nochebuena* or *La Vigilia,* there may be parades, outdoor markets, and visiting. Naturally, the Nativity crèche, first created by Saint Francis of Assisi, is prominently displayed in public squares everywhere.

Everyone enjoys the holiday. English poet John Donne once wrote that Christmas saves the world from "midnight," and its celebration across Europe continues to keep the darkness at bay.

"Better hurry up," he said,
"Christmas Day won't keep!"
Then sitting down
for a moment's rest
The old saint
fell asleep.

Norman Rockwell

Most major illustrators of the day designed Santa postcards. Works of Norman Rockwell appeared on holiday cards, including this one of "the old saint" taking a long-deserved nap.

A number of cards from this period reflect the popular Art Deco look. Elements of this art style, characterized by geometric patterns, bold colors, and often symmetrical designs, are found in these cards.

Christmas is here, Old Top!

THERE .. I BEAT YOU TO IT!

Displaying the country's characteristic dry wit, this British postcard— designed to be mailed out early in the season— chides the intended receiver, "There, I Beat You To It!"

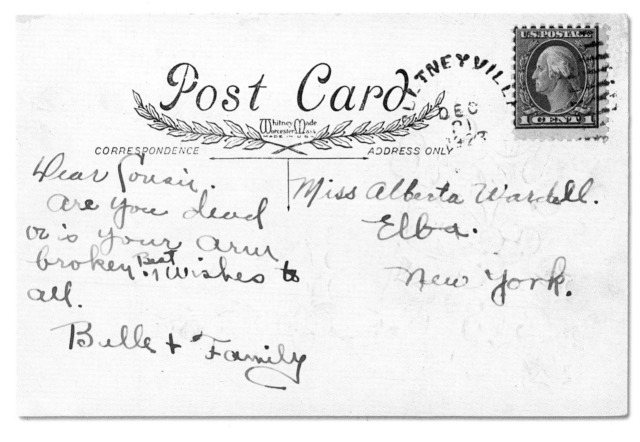

Post Card

Whitney Made
Worcester, Mass
MADE IN U.S.A.

CORRESPONDENCE — ADDRESS ONLY

Dear Cousin.
Are you dead
or is your arm
broken. Best wishes to
all.

Belle & Family

Miss Alberta Warbell.
Elba.
New york.

A JOYFUL   CHRISTMAS
CHRISTMAS DAY IS HERE ONCE MORE
AND ALL THE WORLD IS GLAD,
MAY THIS ONE BE THE MERRIEST
YOU'VE EVER, EVER HAD.

"A Joyful Christmas" poem is featured on this holiday card.

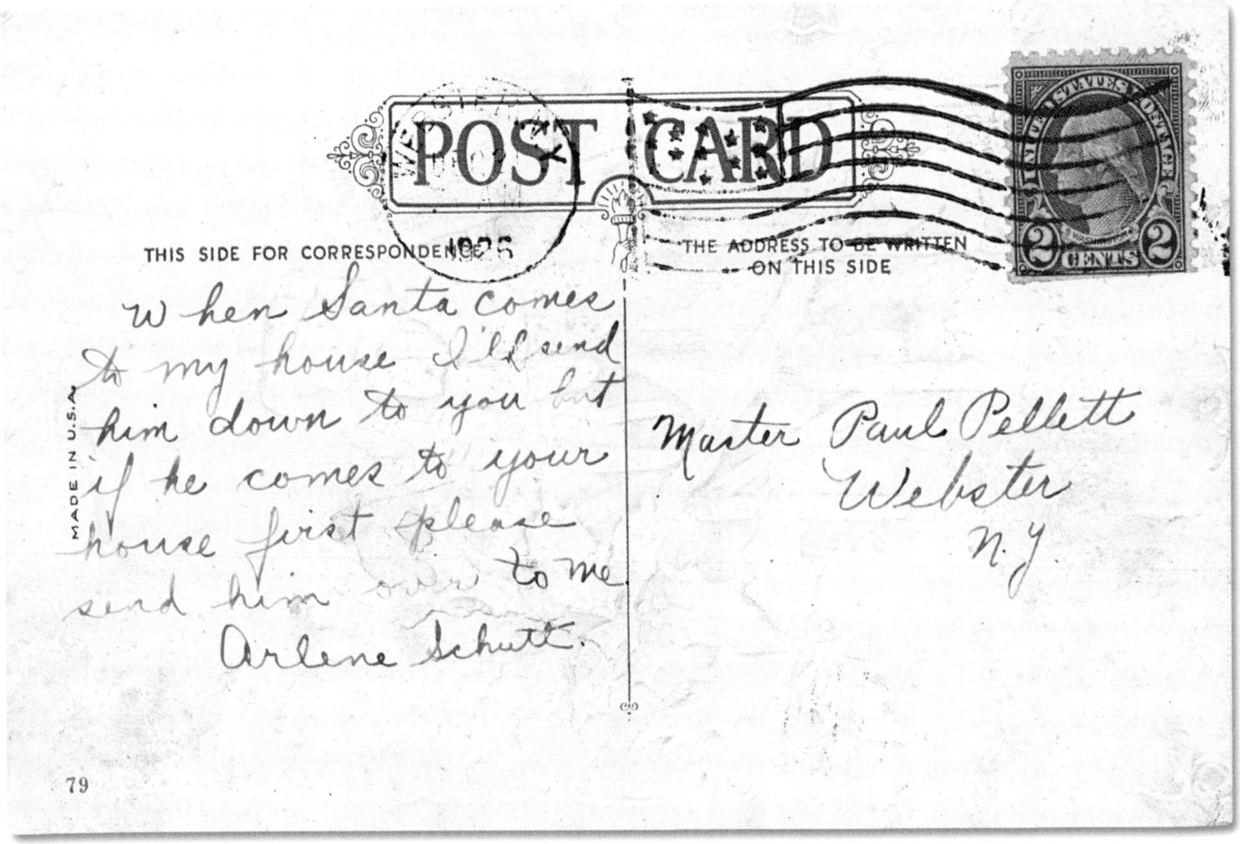
POST CARD
THIS SIDE FOR CORRESPONDENCE
THE ADDRESS TO BE WRITTEN ON THIS SIDE
UNITED STATES POSTAGE
2 CENTS 2
MADE IN U.S.A.
When Santa comes to my house I'll send him down to you but if he comes to your house first please send him over to me
Arlene Schutt
Master Paul Pellett
Webster
N.Y.
79

By the end of the 1930s, Europe was at war and the United States stood poised and ready for involvement.
Postcard messages from Santa often wished for peace on earth.

1:sta pris i
VÄSTGÖTA-KNALLENS
JULBLADS KARIKATYR-
TÄVLING 1938

oscar Sjöberg 1938 -:

In this 1938 postcard, which typified Eastern Europe's long suffering and dim future,
Santa is a skeletal figure who is being pulled on a sled by two small pigs.

Images of Santa Claus

Ever since the sixth century, Europeans have loved Saint Nicholas, even though the gift-giving season initiated by his feast day was tinged with judgment regarding their conduct. Most often pictured as a thin man with a white beard, and carrying a large book where sins and wrongs were recorded, Nicholas sometimes carried a whip or a rod as well as goodies in a sack. Christmas was joyous, but there was always some apprehension attached to Nicholas' arrival.

For centuries, his feast day was universally awaited by European peoples, but after the Protestant Reformation in the sixteenth century, Saint Nicholas' identification with Catholicism caused a change in his role. Several nations developed new, secular gift-giving figures, such as Père Noël of France, Weichnachtsmann of Germany, Jultomten of Scandinavia, and Father Christmas of England. It was the Dutch settlers who brought Saint Nicholas to America, but after years of indifferent pronunciation, his name had become Sinter Klaas. American usage further transformed the name into Santa Claus.

The creation of Santa Claus in the United States was largely a product of nineteenth-century America. Clement C. Moore's 1823 poem "A Visit From St. Nicholas" provided a series of images that were essential to the creation of the Santa we know today (see page 17). Because of the poem's popularity, stockings that hung by the chimney, visions of sugarplums, eight reindeer pulling a sleigh over rooftops, and a pipe-smoking, fur-clad, bearded Saint Nicholas had become elements of the national psyche by the time of the Civil War. However, unlike Saint Nick, Moore's Christmas visitor was a "jolly old elf" who was "small" enough to go up a chimney and drive a "miniature sleigh."

MERRY CHRISTMAS

It was New York City political satirist Thomas Nast, a German immigrant, who gave this beloved Christmas icon life-size stature, transforming him from Saint Nicholas to Santa Claus. Nast provided illustrations for several New York papers before joining the staff of *Harper's Weekly* in 1861. During his career, he drew caricatures of politicians such as "Boss" Tweed, and created party symbols such as the Democratic donkey and the Republican elephant. During the Civil War, his task was to produce "emblematic cartoons," explaining the cause of the North. In December of 1862, Nast drew "Santa Claus in Camp," showing a still elfin Santa giving presents to Union soldiers. Some believe that Nast captured the very idea of Christmas for the North, giving it a distinct advantage in morale over the South.

For the next twenty-three years, Nast created annual Santa Claus woodcuts for *Harper's Weekly,* gradually adding details such as fur trim, pink cheeks, a full beard, a black belt, and the North Pole. Some of Nast's most famous drawings appeared in 1866 and showed Santa decorating a tree, making toys, going over his account books, and searching for good children in his telescope. American children knew instinctively he was eager to bring them presents. In 1880, Nast accepted the job of illustrating yet another edition of "A Visit From St. Nicholas," and two of the major forces in creating America's most celebrated holiday figure came together in triumph. But Nast did not create Mrs. Claus; she was the brainchild of Katherine Lee Bates, a writer who also gave us "America the Beautiful."

Although similar to Saint Nicholas in many ways, Santa is a totally secular figure, a spirit of generosity and fun, and identified with the commercialism that has come to dominate our holiday season. Santa Claus first appeared in Macy's Thanksgiving Day parade in 1924, and ever since, the level of spending for presents often seems to determine how successful the holiday has been. America's most current Santa image is primarily the work of Haddon Sundblom, who, in 1931, drew a full-size, rosy-cheeked salesman who urged us all to drink Coca-Cola.

Whether hawking products or preparing his bag of toys for good little girls and boys, Santa Claus remains a quintessentially American creation whose influence has spread around the entire globe. Long may he reign.

Children spy on Santa as he fills Christmas stockings with goodies in this 1940 prewar postcard.

POST CARD

READING, PA.
DEC 23
5 30 PM
1940

U.S. POSTAGE
ONE CENT

ADDRESS ON THIS SIDE ONLY

425

Thomson Printing Co., 310-312 Cherry St., Phila.

Master Fred Rothermel,
Fifth above Washington,
Reading,
Pa. —

CHAPTER FOUR

Santa Goes to War 1941–1945

By 1941, nations throughout the world were deeply involved in war. Although the United States had maintained a policy of isolationism during the early years of the conflict, Japan's devastating air attack on the naval base at Pearl Harbor in December of 1941, plunged the country headlong into World War II. Interestingly, in the middle of it all—the fighting and the sacrifice—Santa was there. And, as in World War I, his allegiance knew no borders. He supported the war effort in a number of countries, including Russia, China, Canada, England, Italy, Japan, France, Germany, and, of course, the United States.

To some extent, Santa's image in America during the war remained the jovial, eye-twinkling figure it had been in recent years. He was portrayed as a happy and healthy fellow, who was filled with confidence and always ready to flash a smile. Both before and during the war, *National Geographic,* a magazine with one of the largest circulations at that time, featured full-color Coca-Cola advertisements on both its inside front cover and its back cover. Holiday issues frequently featured Haddon Sundblom's famous Santa, who offered supportive messages to G.I. Joes during the war years. Clever, eye-catching ads pictured a happy full-faced, large-bodied Santa offering support to the armed forces. Another magazine that regularly included Santa in its lighthearted, amusing holiday cartoons was *Esquire.* A series of Esky-Cards—postcards of selected cartoons from this periodical—was widely distributed.

The war was on, but Santa still promoted and endorsed merchandise. During the Christmas season, most major magazines featured Santa urging consumers to buy selected products. Gone, however, was the prosperous Santa of the past. Restricted by government rationing and limited spending, he no longer urged consumers to purchase such luxuries as automobiles, expensive jewelry, chocolate, perfume, and nylons. He stopped promoting vacations to destinations throughout the world. Still, with a twinkle in his eye, the World War II Santa encouraged the sale of smaller-ticket items, including wristwatches, radios, hats, cigarettes, and liquor. European Santas were illustrated differently. As conditions deteriorated, he promoted very little. Hard times had put Christmas, Santa, and gift giving on the back burner.

In the United States, Christmas cards and postcards quite often pictured Santa in a military uniform, or offering peaceful wishes within a red, white, and blue patriotic design. Throughout the war, he was commonly depicted backing various activities, but Santa's most important role was his involvement in the government's efforts to win the war. He prompted citizens to bolster the fighting soldier's morale through supportive letters, to help fund the war through the purchase of war bonds, and to conserve critical materials through recycling. He constantly reminded Americans to maintain silence in an effort to prevent critical information leaks to the enemy. On postcards as well as posters, images of Uncle Sam and Santa were often paired for that extra surge of patriotic fervor. A confidant of Presidents Roosevelt and Truman, Santa became a national symbol, and his image remained one of pride, ambition, and invincibility throughout this difficult time.

By the time Christmas arrived in 1945, the war was over. Discharged from his war duties, Santa resumed his more traditional job of delivering gifts to boys and girls throughout the world. His involvement in the war effort had been exhausting, but Santa had done his job of seeing the world through combat and on to better times. 🐦

To keep up the country's morale during the war, Santa continued to be the happy, confident fellow he had always been.

Wishing you a
Merry Christmas
and A Happy New Year

© C. T. & CO.

Merry Christmas
and Happy New Year

© C. T. & CO.

Whether standing on a rooftop or on top of the world, Santa maintained the spirit of Christmas during World War II.

Christmas Greetings from Florida

From Uncle Harry and Aunt Sallie.
721 E. Mc Donald St. Fla.

7A-H3119

Cities and states throughout the country continued using Santa's cheerful face to bid glad tidings of the season.

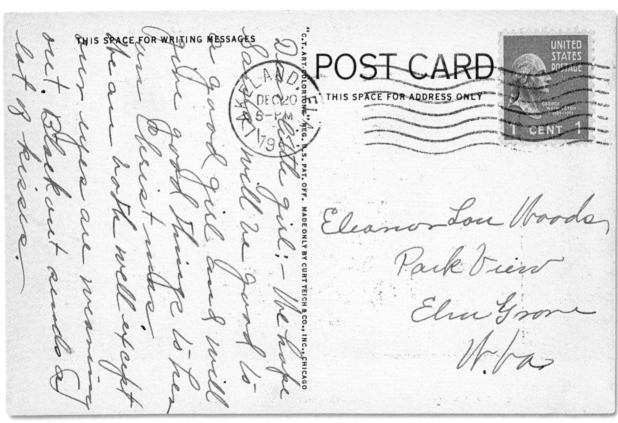

THIS SPACE FOR WRITING MESSAGES

"C.T. ART-COLORTONE." REG. U.S. PAT. OFF. MADE ONLY BY CURT TEICH & CO., INC., CHICAGO

POST CARD

THIS SPACE FOR ADDRESS ONLY

LAKELAND
DEC 20
5-PM
194

UNITED STATES POSTAGE
GEORGE WASHINGTON
1 CENT 1

Eleanor Lou Woods
Park View
Elm Grove
W.Va

Christmas in America

According to *U.S. News and World Report,* 96 percent of all Americans celebrate Christmas in some fashion. Some greet the season at Chanukah and others at Kwanza, but almost all of our citizens attempt to make the season memorable in some way.

The North American colonies were founded after the Protestant Reformation, and in the new religious tradition, Christmas was a Catholic feast day, whose religious meaning was to be ignored. In the first southern colonies, Christmas most often meant a good meal or a hunting expedition; later, it was the only time slaves were permitted to visit relatives on other plantations. But in Puritan New England, its very celebration was a crime. Only the Sabbath was holy, and from 1659 to 1681, celebrations on Christmas Day were absolutely banned. But such a prohibition proved impossible to enforce, and by the early 1700s, the tide had turned in favor of Christmas.

Dutch New Amsterdam taught the other colonies how to greet the season. A statue of Saint Nicholas was erected in its seaport as early as the 1630s, and after the English changed the colony's name to New York, the holiday celebration expanded to fill all the days from December 6 to the new year. Sailors found the holiday a convenient excuse for drinking, and well into the nineteenth century, mobs of lower-class "wassailers" roamed the streets, extorting money from pedestrians and demanding food and drink from homeowners. In fact, it was after a particularly raucous Christmas season in 1828 that the city organized its first police department. City intellectuals such as Washington Irving and Clement Moore denounced such violence, and led efforts to make the holiday more family oriented. Gradually, their influence and the influence of artists and writers such as Thomas Nast and William Garrison tamed the festivities of the season, and the staid Victorian Christmas became commonplace. By the 1870s, Christmas in America had become a "general festival of consumption," a time when friends and family gathered to celebrate over food and drink.

Two other vital holiday elements—the Christmas tree and holiday cards—were introduced during nineteenth-century America. The Christmas tree, first brought to the colonies by German settlers and Hessian soldiers, became common in the 1830s largely due to the efforts of Charles Follen. A Harvard professor, Follen advocated the practice of tree trimming, which spread rapidly in the East. And once Queen Victoria displayed her decorated tree at Windsor Castle in 1848, middle-class Americans everywhere began adopting the ritual. President Franklin Pierce dedicated the first White House tree in

1856, but it wasn't until the tenure of Calvin Coolidge that lights were added in 1923. America's most famous Christmas tree, the extravagant fir that rises yearly in New York's Rockefeller Center, first appeared when construction crews celebrated the season in 1933.

Along with the appearance of decorated trees, the Christmas card heralds the onset of the season in the contemporary United States. It too first appeared in Europe; but in 1875, Louis Prang, an immigrant German lithographer, launched the American version of what is now a worldwide industry. Prang marketed expensive cards decorated with floral designs featuring roses and poinsettias. Within five years, he was selling millions of Christmas cards annually, and the foundation for a year-round greeting card industry was being created. Not surprisingly, the high cost of these cards led most people to exchange only Christmas postcards—at least until the nineteenth century. With the new century, production costs fell and opportunity beckoned. Eighteen-year-old Joyce Hall was one of several new entrants in the greeting card field; today, the firm he established is called Hallmark.

By the early twentieth century, American business had given Christmas a decidedly commercial focus. Two of the nation's favorite toys, the Teddy Bear in 1902 and the Raggedy Ann doll in 1910, were the first in a long line of "must-have" toys that helped usher in the wave of spending that has come to be associated with the holiday. Congress endorsed such commercialism when it legislated an earlier Thanksgiving Day, which lengthened the shopping season.

Stimulation of the economy certainly has become one function of the Christmas season. But in spite of its often commercial atmosphere, Christmas remains the most beloved of all American holidays—a time of reflection, rejoicing, and celebration.

"Come on, Santa Claus, quit acting like the milkman!"

A number of amusing cartoons featured in *Esquire, The Magazine for Men* were reprinted on a series of "Esky-Cards." During the war years, these postcards, as seen in this 1942 example, offered a touch of comic relief to a country at war.

This postcard extends holiday greetings from the Seamen's House—a branch of the YMCA
maintained specifically for the service of the country's "seafaring men."

Postcards from the country's different fighting forces, such as this one from the Army's First Infantry Division—sometimes called the Big Red One—were popular for sending holiday greetings to family and friends back home.

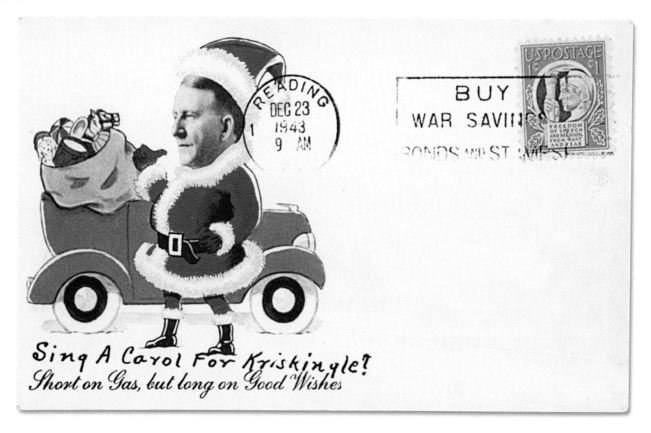

"Short on Gas, but long on Good Wishes," reads this 1943 message from Congressman Guy L. Moser from Pennsylvania. Moser's head replaces Santa's, and he has added the message, "Sing a Carol for Kris Kringle." Note the postmark instruction to BUY WAR SAVINGS BONDS AND STAMPS.

Dear Santa-

Please add Adolph to your bag this year.

This wartime postcard, which was sent by a soldier stationed in Northern Italy (see page 112), depicts a Santa snowman who is given a curious instruction to add Adolph to his gift bag.

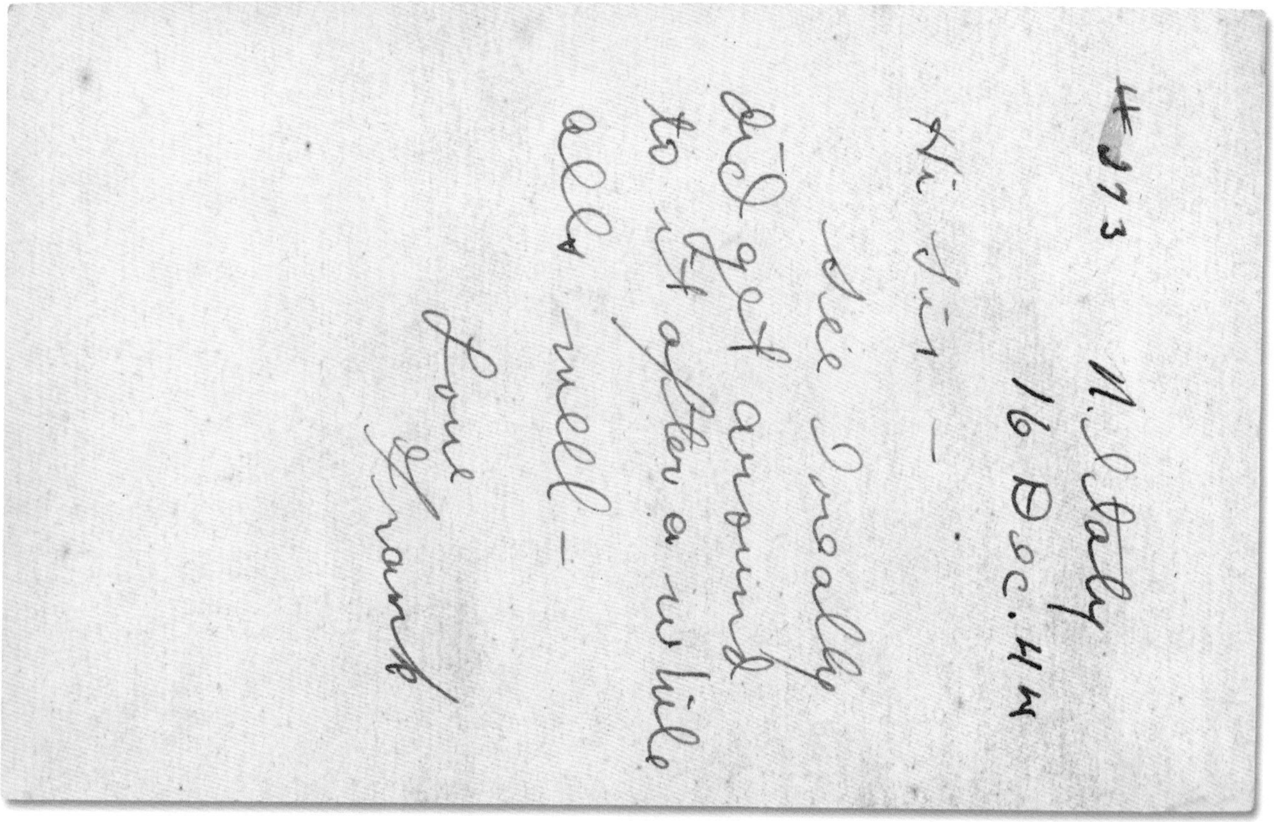
#273 N. Italy
16 Dec. 44

Hi Sis –

See I really
did get around
to it after a while
all's well –

Love
Frank

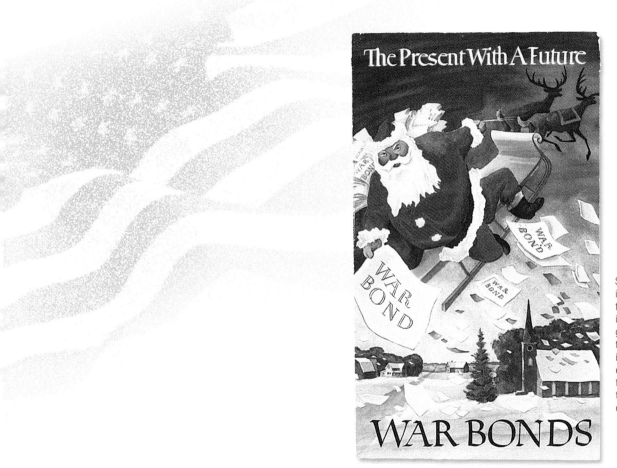

The Present With A Future

WAR BONDS

Santa's most important role during this period was his involvement in the government's efforts to win the war. As seen in this postcard, Santa encourages the country to help fund the conflict through the purchase of war bonds.

Santa's Helpers

What would Santa do without his band of little helpers? Magical elves assist Santa all year long in the North Pole workshop, creating toys and keeping track of the good little girls and boys. In some countries, however, Santa's legendary helpers are not always pleasant, cheerful sprites.

Knecht Ruprecht. In Germany, this famous gnome, whose name in English is Servant Rupert, helps make and distribute gifts. He also keeps track of children who are naughty and nice.

Krampus. Although he is considered a Christmas helper in Austria, this wild-eyed, frightening spirit is more of a boogeyman. He spends cold winter nights searching for naughty children to punish.

Nisse. This Norwegian gnome assists Santa in making presents for good girls and boys. He also keeps track of those who are naughty and nice.

Père Fouettard. In France, this spirit, translated as Father Spanker, is completely different from the kind and generous Père Noël. He is in charge of all naughty children, and punishes them with spankings.

Tontut. This elf-like gnome from Finland helps Santa prepare and distribute toys.

Zwarte Piet. Translated as Black Pete, in Holland, this Moorish helper of Sinter Klaas keeps track of children's behavior. According to legend, Zwarte Piet rewards good children by filling their wooden shoes with sweet treats. He also punishes those who have been naughty by carrying them off in a sack and dumping them in Spain.

Although Santa continued endorsing products during the war years, government rationing and limited spending restricted his promotion of luxuries such as cars, expensive jewelry, and costly vacations. Instead, he encouraged the sale of smaller-ticket items, including wristwatches, radios, hats, cigarettes, and liquor.

Santa encourages customers to buy practical yet inexpensive holiday gifts for men on this Wormser Hat Store postcard.

THE BROOKSIDE RADIO

22^{50}

7405-8

Batteries Extra

Store owners and manufacturers often used inexpensive "stock" postcards for product promotion. In the example above, Santa points to a billboard that advertises a radio, however, this same card could have been used to announce other holiday-type gift items as well.

For the most part, Santa refrained from helping storeowners sell expensive jewelry during World War II, but he continued promoting more essential, everyday items such as wristwatches and wedding rings.

Wishing You
A GREAT BIG LOAD OF
Christmas Cheer
AND A PROSPEROUS AND
Happy New Year

DAILEY'S CHEVROLET
REID W. SPENCER, *Parts & Accessories Sales Mgr.*
1925 State Street   **Phone 26-734**   **Erie, Pa.**

With the war on, limited natural resources such as metal and rubber brought car sales to a standstill.
Car dealerships maintained their businesses through the sale of car parts and servicing.

CHAPTER FIVE

Santa Meets the Baby Boomers 1946–1964

The end of World War II was met with deliriously joyful celebrations throughout the world. In the United States, proud soldiers anxiously returned to a jubilant homeland—one that was about to undergo tremendous changes. Peace would unleash the country's once-restricted buying power, ushering in a period of unparalleled economic growth. Birth rates would skyrocket, the suburbs would be created, and the automobile would become one of life's necessities. During this prosperous postwar period, Santa appeared fit, victorious, happy, and healthy. Budding new families, home ownership, and travel were back in style. The re-emergence of Santa as the "darling of Madison Avenue" was inevitable. More than ever before, Santa became chairman of the board.

The children of the returning soldiers would know the longest period of peacetime prosperity in the history of the nation. They grew up in an era of intense commercialism as new toys and gadgets rolled off assembly lines and headed to neighborhood stores. The enormous number of babies born after World War II—the baby boomers—quickly established Santa Claus as the patron saint of happiness.

During the postwar period, indulgent parents did everything they could to make their children happy. Determined to give them all of the things that they had never had, parents showered their children with the latest toys and gifts. Each December, moms and dads paraded their children to department stores, where the little ones had their pictures taken with Santa. Interestingly, photos with Santa had also been popular during the 1930s with children of the Depression. Because they had nothing, these children considered the activity a special holiday highlight. However, for the indulged generation that followed, this photo opportunity was but one holiday treat in the midst of many—another sign that the baby boomers "had it all."

Travel, both at home and abroad, was once again both feasible and encouraged. Countries once deemed off-limits or simply out of reach began to solicit tourism, and Santa was there to help. His face appeared on numerous postcards for airlines and travel agencies, encouraging trips and vacations. Santa also tried to made travel easier by promoting car sales. Car dealers of all makes and models relied on Santa to help bring in customers. He also assisted presidents, mayors, congressmen, and other political figures whenever he was needed. Republicans and Democrats alike counted on him as their special helper. He supported blood drives for the American Red Cross, encouraged the sale of Christmas Seals for the American Lung Association, and promoted fundraisers of all types, particularly those for the benefit of children. Santa was always available to lend a helping hand.

The 1950s saw the rise of Santa tourist attractions—enchanting re-creations of North Pole workshops and model villages complete with helpful elves, live reindeer, and Santa himself. Located in places like North Pole, New York; Santa Claus, California; Christmas, Michigan; and North Pole, Alaska, these family attractions were open twelve months of the year. Thousands of Santa souvenirs, including postcards, were sold at these sites, and have become collectibles over time. Even Santa Claus training schools were established!

Famous personalities like Elvis Presley, Mickey Mantle, and the Mickey Mouse Club Mousekateers, as well as characters like Howdy Doody and Davy Crockett, delighted baby boomers and their doting parents. These and other popular figures made live appearances with Santa during the 1950s and early 1960s, and were pictured with him on posters and postcards, as well as books, calendars, and other collectibles.

Over time, members of this generation would become ardent collectors of Santa Claus memorabilia. In large part, this can be attributed directly to the intense level of marketing that had been aimed at them during their childhood. Add the romanticizing of the nuclear family that occurred during the 1950s and 1960s, and the result was a generation that viewed Christmas as a feel-good, if highly commercialized, holiday. Advertising campaigns, reminders to shop early, Christmas-in-July sales, and the making of movies with Santa in a starring role, helped keep this beloved Christmas figure alive in everyone's mind. ❧

Holiday Greetings to You All *from* **Elvis** and the Colonel

Famous personalities of the day were often pictured with Santa on posters, postcards, and other collectibles. Elvis Presley fans were treated to this holiday postcard of the "King" while he was in the service. A "telegram message" from Elvis is found on the back (see page 122).

WESTERN WESTERN WESTERN
UNION   UNION   UNION

WUAO2O 72 PD INTL
CD BADNAUHEIM VIA RCA NOV 5 1936
LT COLONEL TOM PARKER
WUX MADISON (TENN)

DEAR FANS: MANY OF YOU ASK FOR A NEW RECORD. `SO

THAT MY CAREER WOULD NOT INTERFERE WITH MY ARMY DUTY

I DID NOT RECORD IN GERMANY. I WILL DO MY BEST TO

HAVE A NEW RECORD SOON AS I RETURN. THANKS TO ALL

OF YOU ALSO THE DISC JOCKEYS RECORD DEALERS

DISTRIBUTORS AND RCA VICTOR FOR MAKING THIS MESSAGE

POSSIBLE

SINCERELY YOUR PAL

ELVIS PRESLEY

850AMC NOV 6.

WESTERN WESTERN WESTERN
UNION   UNION   UNION

Copy Telegram From Elvis to the Colonel for his Fans

PLACE
STAMP
HERE

Favorite television and cartoon characters began appearing on holiday postcards, much to the delight of children everywhere.

Santa's Sleigh

Have you ever wondered
Where Santa leaves his sleigh,
When he brings toys for girls
    and boys
To find on Christmas Day?

For reindeer, all the rooftops
Are much too smooth and steep!
One slip, and they'll go sliding down,
And land in one big heap!

But if they were in the garden,
How could Santa, with his sack,
Climb right up to the rooftop,
Then down the chimney stack?

There's too much danger in the road.
So, where CAN he leave his sleigh?
Perhaps you'd like to ask him,
When he comes round your way.

—Author Unknown

With the war over, international travel was promoted once again. This 1960 Swedish postcard from SAS airlines pictures a joyful Santa amidst a group of children from all over the world.

Santa, Sinter, Père Noël

Santa is a beloved figure throughout the world. He is known by the following names in different countries:

FRANCE *Père Noël*

CHINA *Shengdan Laoren*

HOLLAND *Sinter Klaas*

GERMANY *Weihnachtsmann*

ITALY *Belfana*

SWEDEN *Jultomten*

ENGLAND *Father Christmas*

PERU *Papa Noel*

FINLAND *Joulupukki*

RUSSIA *Grandfather Frost*

Greetings from

Santa Claus House

SANTALAND

North Pole, Alaska

The 1950s saw the rise of Santa tourist attractions—enchanting re-creations of North Pole workshops and model villages complete with helpful elves, live reindeer, and Santa himself. This postcard hails from the Santa Claus House in North Pole, Alaska.

Santa and his helpers feed one of the reindeer at Fantasyland in Gettysburg, Pennsylvania.

Santa and His helpers - Fantasyland, Gettysburg, Pa.

Small Visitors Chatting with Santa Claus, Santa Claus Land, Santa Claus, Indiana

OC304-N

In 1927, Santa Fe, Indiana was renamed Santa Claus, Indiana. It has the only Santa Claus Post Office in the United States from which millions of cards and letters have been officially postmarked. In this postcard, Santa is surrounded by young visitors at this city's Santa Claus Land.

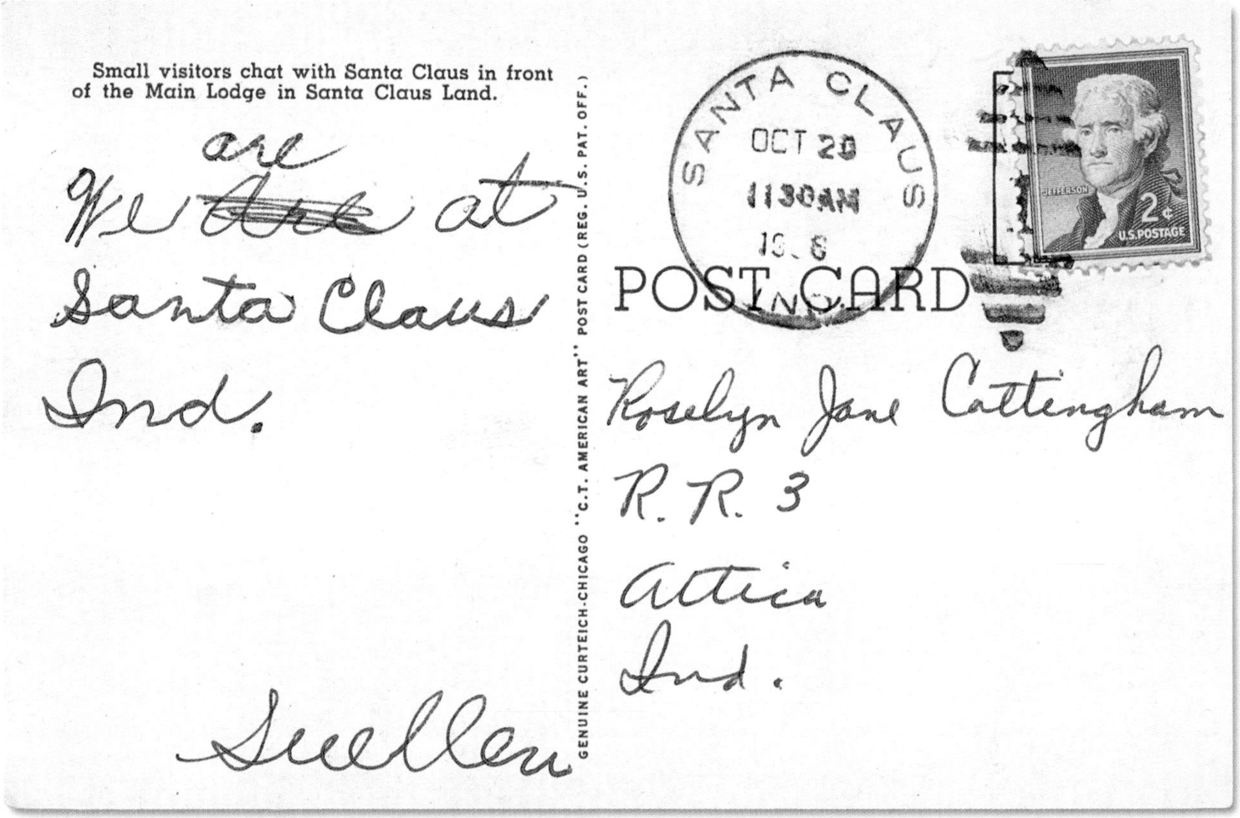

Small visitors chat with Santa Claus in front
of the Main Lodge in Santa Claus Land.

are
We ~~are~~ at
Santa Claus
Ind.

Suellen

POST CARD

SANTA CLAUS
OCT 20
11 30 AM
19 6

Roselyn Jane Cattingham
R. R. 3
Attica
Ind.

GENUINE CURTEICH-CHICAGO "C.T. AMERICAN ART" POST CARD (REG. U.S. PAT. OFF.)

Santa is found all year round at Christmas tourist attractions like Santa's Village in Jefferson, New Hampshire.

Santa's elves are pictured in front of his house at Santa's Village in Jefferson, New Hampshire.
They are responsible for running Santa's workshop, gift shop, and post office at this popular tourist attraction.

SANTA CLAUS, CALIFORNIA

Delightful shops and restaurants on Santa Claus Lane make for an interesting tourist stop in Santa Claus, California.

"Wanna be" Santas from all over the country gathered at the Santa Claus School in Albion, New York, where they received special training in the art of playing that jolly old elf.

Christmas Seals

For nearly a century, the holiday season has been associated with the brightly colored stamps known as Christmas Seals. But while they are used to adorn both Christmas mail and packages, these seals do more than add a touch of color and a cheerful holiday motif to postcards, letters, and gifts. Here is their story . . .

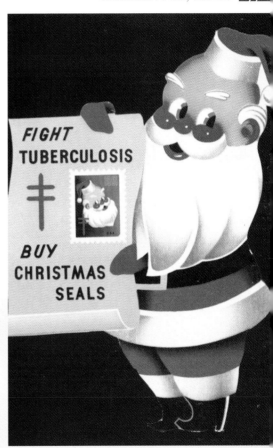

In the early 1900s, tuberculosis, known as the "White Plague," was one of the most feared diseases in the world. There was no cure for TB, but it had been found that complete rest in quiet, peaceful surroundings could lead to recovery. As a result, sanatoriums offering "rest cures" had sprung up all over the world. The problem was that the funds available for these facilities were inadequate to aid the many victims of the disease, and most sanatoriums were makeshift and could serve only a few patients.

In 1907, one such sanatorium, situated on the banks of the Brandywine River in Delaware, faced a severe money shortage. It was, in fact, about to close its doors when one of the doctors, Joseph Wales, approached his cousin Emily Bissell, asking for help. Because Emily had successfully raised funds for the American Red Cross, Dr. Wales hoped that his cousin could "find a way" to keep the doors of the sanatorium open.

Anxious to help, Emily remembered an article she had read about a fund-raising effort in Denmark. There, special Christmas seals had been sold in post offices around the country for a half-penny apiece, with the result that two new Danish TB hospitals had been built. Inspired, Emily quickly sketched a design of a red cross centered on a half-wreath of holly above the words "Merry Christmas." Then, with the help of a forty-dollar

loan, she had 50,000 seals printed, and arranged to have them sold at a stand in the Wilmington, Delaware post office for a penny apiece. The seals were placed in small envelopes, each of which bore the following words:

25 Christmas Stamps one penny apiece
issued by the Delaware Red Cross
to stamp out the White Plague.

Put this stamp with message bright
On every Christmas letter;
Help the tuberculosis fight,
And make the New Year better.

These stamps do not carry any kind of mail
but any kind of mail will carry them.

Although sales were at first slow, Emily worked hard to rally support. With the help of leading newspapers, who urged the public to "Stamp Out Tuberculosis," as well as from high public officials such as President Theodore Roosevelt, the campaign became nationwide. Word soon spread that TB could be beaten, and that the pennies paid for Christmas Seals could add up to the dollars needed to vanquish the White Plague. By the time the holiday season had come to an end, $3,000 had been raised—ten times the amount needed to keep the doors of the Brandywine facility open.

Today, the American Lung Association mails out both Christmas Seals and Chanukah Seals to thousands of people across the country. The seals are now free of charge, however, like the original stamps, they are designed to promote awareness of the association's mission—to offer help and hope to those who suffer from lung disease. What better way is there to express the true spirit of the holiday season?

The Season's Best

Christmas Gift!

In appreciation of your friendship for
Coca-Cola, let us make you a
present of this carton of six to enjoy at home

Just present this card (and a carton of empty bottles
or usual deposit) to the dealer of your choice
and get your full carton with our compliments and best wishes.

Note to Dealer: Our salesman will redeem this card.

This offer
Expires
Jan. 1

A postcard that doubles as a gift card for a six-pack of Coca-Cola bears the image of Haddon Sundblom's famous Santa Claus.

This 1954 Christmas-gift postcard confirms a subscription to the *Democratic Digest*.

Car sales skyrocketed during the postwar period, and dealers relied on Santa's expert salesmanship to help bring in customers. This special postcard in which Santa promotes the 1956 Ford Fairlane is actually a 78 RPM record (see page 140).

This is a Special Record
by Rosemary Clooney
and Mitch Miller's Orchestra

Play it on any standard "78 RPM" phonograph machine and take Rosemary's advice for Christmas enjoyment and year-round satisfaction.

Here's your chance to get in tune with the deal of a lifetime which I can get f you. See and drive the '56 Ford tod Your whole family will love Ford's Thunderbird Power and Styling and you can travel all the New Year with Ford's new Lifeguard Design.

Why don't you come in now for the buy of your life!

John R Lough
Salesman

OTTMAN MOTORS
COOPERSTOWN, N.Y.

Columbia Records New York 19, N. Y.

An "AURAVISION" Production By

COOPERSTOWN
DEC
4 P
1955
N. Y.

2¢ JEFFERSON U.S. POSTAGE

RD #1
Milford
NY

Joyeux Noël

During World War II, most countries throughout Europe had placed holiday merriment on the back burner. But when the war ended, the Christmas season was once again a time for celebration. Santa resumed his place as the joyful symbol of peace and happiness, as seen in this 1955 French postcard of Père Noël.

С НОВЫМ ГОДОМ!

Less than 15 percent of Russians celebrate Christmas on December 25, but millions more exchange gifts on New Year's Day or on Orthodox Christmas Day in early January.

CHAPTER SIX

Modern-Day Santa 1965–Millennium

Santa Claus' appearance throughout the second half of the twentieth century and into the millennium has remained largely unchanged. This modern-day Santa, who made his debut in a series of illustrious Coca-Cola ads by artist Haddon Sundblom in the 1930s, was a fine-tuned version of the earlier creation by illustrator Thomas Nast. Ever the plump, grandfatherly gent with a twinkle in his eye, the new Santa, who was still clad in a signature fur-trimmed red suit, looked more like a real person than Nast's character. His new natural look made Santa more human and more believable than ever before.

For the most part, postcards were no longer used to send personal greetings of the season. Holiday sentiments and good wishes for the coming year were conveyed primarily through holiday greeting cards, which came in a range of shapes, sizes, and prices, and had to be placed in envelopes before mailing. However, Santa himself remained as popular as ever and continued to appear on hundreds of items ranging from wrapping paper and T-shirts to backpacks and dinnerware. The majority of Santa postcards that were issued during this period were used for advertisements and promotions. Santa Claus theme parks, villages, and amusement centers throughout the country always had plenty of these postcards on hand as inexpensive souvenirs. And to encourage tourism, cities often printed cards on which a happy Santa beckoned the public to visit. Scores of paparazzi lovers—politicians and actors, sports figures and musicians— enjoyed posing with dear old Santa, and appeared with him on many promotional postcards. Furthermore, many celebrities themselves, in the lighthearted spirit of the season, donned Santa outfits and posed as this beloved figure for fundraisers, charitable events, or just plain fun.

Although a number of artists and cartoonists of the day offered renderings of Santa during this time, photographs or computerized designs were used on most postcards. The advent of computer graphics and electronic imaging in the late 1980s allowed unlimited artistic interpretations of Santa, who, with the click of a mouse, could be easily placed in a variety of situations. From work or home, anyone could design and print original postcards, greeting cards, and banners with ease. Long gone were the intricate, detailed illustrations that characterized postcards of past generations.

At the end of the twentieth century, an entire generation of baby boomers began to enter their fifties. As they aged, so did their increasing desire to recapture childhood memories. With their growing nostalgia, appreciation for all things old and vintage increased as well. Beautifully crafted postcards from the Victorian era and turn-of-the-century America became highly sought-after collectibles. Santa items—both old and new—were in demand, and their popularity grew as baby boomers continued to mature.

Christmas shops that offered collectibles began popping up throughout the United States and in countries all over the world. Santa items of all kinds, including postcards and message cards—both originals and reproductions—were available all year long. In addition to these holiday shops, growing numbers of clubs, organizations, and publications for collectors, as well as online auction houses and holiday Internet sites, made it easy to hunt down Santa treasures.

No matter what circumstance or under what condition he makes his appearance, Santa has a special way of helping make us a little bit happier each time we see him. Always our treasured friend, Santa continues to symbolize joy, generosity, and the enduring value of our most cherished traditions. 🖎

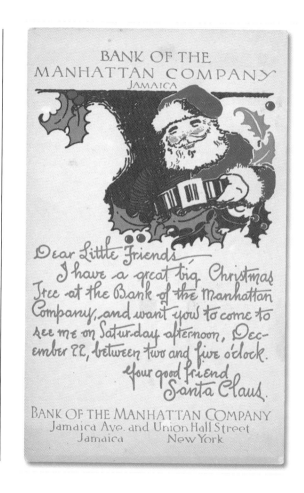

HO!HO!HO!

MERRY CHRISTMAS

In the lighthearted spirit of the season, celebrities and other well-known persons donned Santa outfits and posed as this beloved figure for fundraisers, charitable events, or just plain fun. President Ronald Reagan and actor Harry Morgan (M*A*S*H's Colonel Sherman Potter) portray Santa in these postcards from the early 1980s.

First Lady Nancy Reagan stands next to Santa Claus (John Riggins of the Washington Redskins) during a 1984 children's Christmas party at the White House.

"Say, didn't I see you on a TV commercial in another role?"

R. BAKER

Holly

R. Baker's cartoon rendering on the left exemplifies commercialism at its best, while the card on the right presents a more traditional portrayal of a child and Santa.

holiday Songs with Santa

For most of us, Christmas songs are an important part of the festive season. Perhaps you play carols during your holiday festivities, and perhaps you even sing them with family and friends. If so, you might want to include a few songs that mention Father Christmas himself. Not all the lyrics are reverent. (Santa has been known to kiss Mommy under the mistletoe, and even to run over Grandma.) But all are sure to add to the fun of the occasion and to remind you of the jolly old man who represents the spirit of the season.

- ♪ **"The Christmas Song"** *(Chestnuts roasting on an open fire . . .)* by Mel Torme and Robert Wells

- ♪ **"Grandma Got Run Over by a Reindeer"** by Randy Brooks (1977)

- ♪ **"Here Comes Santa Claus"** by Gene Autry and Oakley Haldeman (1947)

- ♪ **"I'm Gettin' Nuttin' for Christmas"** by S. Tepper and R. Bennett (1955)

- ♪ **"I Saw Mommy Kissing Santa Claus"** by J.T. Connor (1952)

- ♪ **"Jolly Old Saint Nicholas"**

- ♪ **"Rudolph the Red-Nosed Reindeer"** by Johnny Marks (1949)

- ♪ **"Santa, Baby"** by J. Javits and P. Springer

- ♪ **"Santa Claus Is Coming to Town"** by J. Fred Coots and Henry Gillespie (1934)

- ♪ **"Silver Bells"** by Ray Evans and Jay Livingston

- ♪ **"Up on the Housetop"** by B.R. Hanby

Santa's Lap

This "singing" postcard of the early 1960s is actually a 45 RPM record that plays "Rudolph the Red-Nosed Reindeer," a holiday favorite.

I like to visit Santa Claus
When Christmastime is near.
It's fun to climb up on his lap
And whisper in his ear.

He says, "My dear, have you been good?
Have you done what Mother said you should?
Do you brush your teeth and hair each day?
Are you kind to others when you play?"

I listen to each question
And answer every one.
Although I am ashamed to say
I must say no to some.

But Santa never scares me;
He doesn't even scold.
He just says, "Try again, my dear,
You're a fine lad, I am told."

—Author Unknown

In this French postcard, Santa races to light the torch for the 1992 winter Olympic Games held in Albertville, France.

Santa spells out a 1981 Christmas greeting in the sands of a tranquil Hawaiian beach.

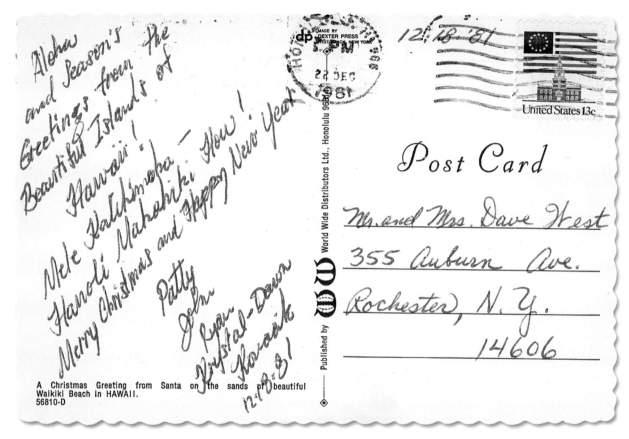

Aloha and Season's Greetings from the Beautiful Islands of Hawaii!

Mele Kalikimaka — Hauoli Makahiki Hou! Merry Christmas and Happy New Year!

Patty
John
Ryan-Dawn
Krystal-Dawn
Novaak
12/18/81

A Christmas Greeting from Santa on the sands of beautiful Waikiki Beach in HAWAII.
56810-D

Published by World Wide Distributors Ltd., Honolulu 96814

MADE BY DEXTER PRESS WEST NYACK, NEW YORK

12/18/81

United States 13c

POST CARD

Mr. and Mrs. Dave West
355 Auburn Ave.
Rochester, N.Y.
14606

Santa the horticulturist tends to his holiday plants in this postcard from the 1970s.

In 1960, the Steiff Company toy manufacturer used this postcard to advertise Santa's reindeer—the latest addition to its line of "Zoo Favorites."

Santa Goes Hollywood

The following movies feature that "jolly old elf," and can be counted among some of Hollywood's holiday favorites.

A Christmas Story (1983). Heartwarming story based on the memoirs of humorist Jean Shepherd, who grew up in the 1940s. In it, the main character, Ralphie, wants Santa to bring him a Red Ryder B-B gun for Christmas.

All I Want for Christmas (1991). With a little Christmas magic from Santa Claus, a brother and sister team manages to get their divorced parents back together.

The Christmas That Almost Wasn't (1965). Attorney Sam Whipple teams with Santa to prevent Phineas Prune, who holds the deed to the North Pole and is demanding back rent, from evicting Santa, Mrs. Claus, and the elves.

Ernest Saves Christmas (1988). Bumbling, well-meaning Ernest tries to help Santa find a successor or else there won't be Christmas.

How the Grinch Stole Christmas (2000). Based on the Dr. Seuss book, this magical tale is about a nasty creature who hates Christmas and tries to steal it away from the Whos of Whoville.

Miracle on 34th Street (1947, 1973, 1994). Beloved holiday classic in which Kris Kringle, working in Macy's Department Store, goes on trial to prove he's Santa Claus.

The Nightmare Before Christmas (1993). Ghoulishly animated tale of Jack Skellington—Pumpkin King and ruler of Halloweentown. He happens upon Christmastown, and decides to change Christmas into another Halloween. He kidnaps Santa Claus, and then delivers some un-Christmaslike gifts to the town's children.

One Magic Christmas (1985). Disney movie about a woman who loses the Christmas spirit during hard times, but with the help of her daughter, her guardian angel, and Santa, she gets it back.

Prancer (1989). Sentimental story about an eight-year-old farm girl who nurses a wounded reindeer she believes is one of Santa's.

Santa Claus (1899). In this very short, black-and-white silent film, Santa Claus enters the room from the fireplace, trims the tree, and fills the stockings that hang on the mantle. He quickly darts back to the fireplace and disappears up the chimney.

Santa Claus: The Movie (1985). When aging Santa Claus needs some help in getting his toys to all the children of the world, his two best elves have a contest to see who gets to be his helper.

The Santa Clause (1994). When a neglectful dad frightens Santa off his roof, accidentally killing him, he finds himself magically recruited to take Santa's place.

This British card, which predates the fall of Communism in Russia, is an example of the Brits' wry sense of humor. In an effort to convey the message that people are people regardless of their political beliefs, Karl Marx is dressed up as Santa Claus. The back of the card reads, "At Christmas, Marxists are just as nice as Christians."

THE ONLY OTHER OVERNIGHT SERVICE THAT DELIVERS ON CHRISTMAS.

Our sleighs deliver at no extra charge on weekends and holidays and can put 8 ounces under anybody's tree for just $9.95.

EXPRESS MAIL

Season's Greetings

The United States Postal Service relies on Santa to promote its Express Mail overnight delivery service, while The Coca-Cola Company uses him to advertise a small soft-drink office dispenser.

Although photos and computerized images of Santa were used on most postcards of this period, a number of artistic renderings made their way into the mix as well. This late twentieth-century card offers a watercolor interpretation of Santa Claus by artist Nancy Poes.

Conclusion

Ever since Santa Claus was first introduced to the world, he has been viewed as a symbol of warmth, generosity, and joy. An endearing magical figure, he somehow manages, by his mere presence, to narrow generation gaps and brighten cold, dark Decembers. Through his own benevolent gestures, Santa has taught people everywhere the importance of kindness and giving.

Although his humble beginnings can be traced back to Saint Nicholas, the generous fourth-century bishop, Santa Claus is actually an early American creation. Introduced to the world in 1823 through Clement Moore's classic holiday poem, Santa's poetic image was further developed through the artistry of Thomas Nast in the 1860s, and then fine-tuned through a series of clever advertisements for Coca-Cola by artist Haddon Sundblom in the 1930s.

Along with written messages, Santa's image on over a century of postcards has helped document his changing role throughout the years. Watching him grow and evolve has been an interesting journey, and a reflection of our own lives. Whether a holiday gift giver, master salesman, politician, or symbol of hope, his fascination cannot be denied. Santa's special image remains alive in the hearts and minds of people everywhere—a joyful reminder of the purity and innocence of youth.

So we thank you, Mr. Moore, Mr. Nast, and Mr. Sundblom, for your contributions, just as we thank all the thousands of artists who have given us Santas who are jolly or serene, plump or thin, reverent or whimsical. Each of you is responsible for helping create this joyful character, and for that, we are forever grateful.

The Messages in Print

For the purpose of clarity, each of the handwritten messages found on the postcards has been transcribed and appears below. Minimal clarifications have been made, and are denoted by brackets.

Page 27. *Dear Santa, I am a little girl eight years old. I am at my Granmothers house and I want a sweetheart braclet, pair of white boot and lots of candy, nuts. And don't forget my sister, she is six years old and then there is my little brother he wants a train and that is all. / Lovingly yours, Judy*

Page 32. *As I could'nt get to see you this year, I am sending you a little gift and my photograph on this card. Don't you think I look natural? / Lovingly, Santa Claus*

Page 35. *My Dear Son I hope this letter finds you well. Father and I are as well as can be expected. We look forward to your visit in the Spring and are counting the days until we get to see our new grandson. / Love, Mother*

Page 36. *My Dear Son I thank you for your morning robe it is nice & warm I wear it every morning Joseph and wife were here yesterday [on] their anniversary we are doing as well as we know how we will send you something soon / Mother*

Page 46. *Dear Little Friend, Your very nice letter has reached me through the Children's Editor of the Baltimore News. I have entered in my Big Book a list of the things you wish. Be good and I will do my best to leave something for you on Christmas. / With much love, Santa Claus*

Page 50. *Does our Santa Look good to you. he does to me and the other kids. / Max*

Page 52. *This is a place on the river a little ways from here I have fished many times along here My wife caught a 4 1/2 [pound] trout down by the little house you can see in the picture Old Snake River is noted for its fine fishing The ferry crosses the river to Heises hot springs at the house in the picture / WLD*

Page 62. *Dear Cousin, say are you getting as sick of waiting for Santa Clause as I am I wish the old bugger would come I want to see if he brings what I wrote for ans[wer] soon. / Ernest*

Page 80. *Dear Grandma Kein: To wish you a Merry Christmas & may the New Year bring you untold happiness & pleasure. We are all well here. Sister & I were down town with Daddy a few days ago, and we were in the Boston Store & there was a Santa and a little pony there so Sister I had some photos made and we are sending this one to you. With lots of love & best wishes from each of us here. / Lovingly your Grandson & Granddaughter, Calvin D. Jr. & Little Frances Yvonne.*

Page 90. *Dear Cousin, Are you dead or is your arm broken. Best wishes to all. / Belle & Family*

Page 92. *When Santa comes to my house I'll send him down to you but if he comes to your house first please send him over to me. / Arlene Schutt*

Page 98. *Here's Santa Claus caught in the act—I'm afraid he doesn't like it! / Affectionately, H. Mary Cushman*

Page 104. *Dear little girl: - We hope Santa will be good to a good girl and will give good things to her on Christmas. We are both well except our eyes are wearing out. Blackout sends a lot of kisses.*

Page 112. *Hi Sis - See I really did get around to it [writing] after a while. Alls well / Love Frank*

Page 122. *DEAR FANS: MANY OF YOU ASK FOR A NEW RECORD. SO THAT MY CAREER WOULD NOT INTERFERE WITH MY ARMY DUTY, I DID NOT RECORD IN GERMANY. I WILL DO MY BEST TO HAVE A NEW RECORD SOON AS I RETURN. THANKS TO ALL OF YOU ALSO THE DISC JOCKEYS RECORD DEALERS DISTRIBUTORS AND RCA VICTOR FOR MAKING THIS MESSAGE POSSIBLE. SINCERELY YOUR PAL / ELVIS PRESLEY*

Page 130. *We are at Santa Claus Ind. / Suellen*

Page 152. *Aloha and Season's Greetings from the Beautiful Islands of Hawaii! Mele Kalikimaka—Hauoli Makahiki Hou! Merry Christmas and Happy New Year. / Patty, John, Ryan, Krystal-Dawn Kovacik*

Index

All numbers that appear in blue type indicate pages that include postcard images.

OTHER POSTCARD BOOKS *from* SQUAREONE PUBLISHERS

POSTCARDS FROM TIMES SQUARE by George J. Lankevich

Through 130 postcards that span a century, *Postcards from Times Square* paints a picture of an area that has been the home of movie palaces and playhouses, of elite restaurants and fast-food chains, and, eventually, of the best-known New Year's celebration in the world. You'll see the Great White Way exchange its gaslights for electric bulbs and, eventually, for neon. You'll visit famed sights like Roseland, Radio City Music Hall, and Sardi's. And you'll discover how this world-renowned landmark has weathered a tumultuous century, growing from its rural roots, achieving worldwide fame, suffering a twilight of decay, and, ultimately, recapturing its magic.

$14.95 • 192 pages • 8.5 x 5.5-inch quality paperback • NYC/Collectibles/History • ISBN 0-7570-0100-9

POSTCARDS FROM MANHATTAN by George J. Lankevich

Through authentic postcard images and messages, *Postcards from Manhattan* takes you on a guided tour of New York old and new. Arranged by region, 120 beautiful postcards show the evolution of seven distinct areas of the city: the tip of Manhattan, lower Manhattan, midtown Manhattan, upper Manhattan, Central Park, the East Side, and the West Side. You'll visit lost New York, where magnificent hotels like the Astor pampered the rich and famous. You'll see the changing face of landmarks like Pennsylvania Station and Madison Square Garden. And you'll view sights that continue to attract visitors today.

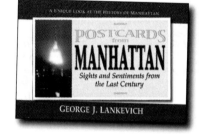

$14.95 • 192 pages • 8.5 x 5.5-inch quality paperback • NYC/Collectibles/History • ISBN 0-7570-0101-7

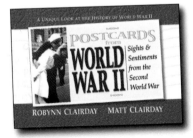

POSTCARDS FROM WORLD WAR II by Robynn Clairday and Matt Clairday

Postcards from World War II offers an invaluable collection of postcards that were sent between 1941 and 1945. Through their images and messages, these cards offer a unique glimpse into the everyday lives of the servicemen and women who lived during this historic fight for freedom. The postcard was a quick, convenient means for soldiers to communicate with distant loved ones, and no matter what the message, each card was a way of saying, "I'm okay." In a world of doubt and devastation, it was an affirmation of life. *Postcards from World War II* helps recapture the triumphs and the tragedies of this time. Each postcard is truly a part of our collective American history, a tangible memory of the heroism of the "greatest" generation.

$14.95 • 192 pages • 8.5 x 5.5-inch quality paperback • Collectibles/History • ISBN 0-7570-0102-5